READING AND WRITING
IN THE PRIMARY GRADES

The Authors

Maryann Murphy Manning and Gary L. Manning are Professors in the School of Education at the University of Alabama at Birmingham. They are the authors of *Reading Instruction in the Middle School, Improving Spelling in the Middle Grades,* and *A Guide and Plan for Conducting Reading (K-12) In-Service Workshops,* published by NEA; and the editors of *Reading K-12: The NEA In-Service Training Program.*

Roberta Long is a Professor in the School of Education at the University of Alabama at Birmingham.

Bernice J. Wolfson is a Professor in the School of Education at the University of Alabama at Birmingham.

The Advisory Panel

Freyda M. Craw, Speech/Language Pathologist, Salem, Massachusetts

Guy Priest, teacher, Chauncey Davis Elementary School, South Bend, Washington

Marjorie B. Weest, Speech Pathologist, Havertown, Pennsylvania

READING AND WRITING IN THE PRIMARY GRADES

A Whole-Language View

Maryann Murphy Manning, Gary L. Manning
Roberta Long, and Bernice J. Wolfson

nea PROFESSIONAL LIBRARY
National Education Association
Washington, D.C.

Authors' Acknowledgment

Our appreciation is expressed to Constance Kamii for her contribution to our understanding of constructivism and for her assistance in the development of the model of Language Arts in the Construction of Knowledge.

Printing History
    First Printing: August 1987
    Second Printing: February 1991
    Third Printing: September 1991

Note

The opinions expressed in this publication should not be construed as representing the policy or position of the National Education Association. Materials published as part of the Analysis and Action Series are intended to be discussion documents for teachers who are concerned with specialized interests of the profession.

Library of Congress Cataloging-in-Publication Data

Reading and writing in the primary grades.

   (Analysis and action series)
   Bibliography: p.
   1. Language arts (Primary)—United States.
2. Reading (Primary)—Language experience approach.
3. Literary—United States.   I. Manning, Maryann Murphy.
II. Series
LB1529.U5R43   1987   372.6   87–21989
ISBN 0-8106-1697-1

CONTENTS

INTRODUCTION

Why are some classrooms heavy with boredom and apathy and others lively, exciting, and vibrant? For decades, research studies have found that it's the *teacher* who makes the difference. Few people would question this conclusion but the seminal question still remains. Why do some teachers inspire children's learning and others stifle it? It depends, we believe, on the assumptions teachers have about knowledge and how it is constructed, the understandings they have about teaching and learning, and how children grow and develop as literacy learners.

This publication is based on (1) the Piagetian theory that knowledge, even social knowledge (including reading and writing), is constructed by each individual, and (2) the psycholinguistic view of literacy that learning takes place best when viewed as holistic and when instructional materials for children are authentic and purposeful.

In this publication, we describe our concepts and the ideas of other teachers and researchers who focus on the constructive nature of children's thinking, reading and writing, and the natural development of these processes. In Chapter 1, we discuss a model of literacy learning and the role of teachers in creating sound literacy programs for their pupils, and in Chapters 2 and 3, we present instructional practices that support the natural literacy development of young children. We include only those practices that are consistent with what has become known as a *whole-language* approach to literacy development.

One of the most basic assumptions of the whole-language approach provides the theme of our publication—*reading and writing in school should be natural and enjoyable for children*. Teachers can create environments where children use reading and writing in ways that are authentic and meaningful. Instead of directing children to copy exercises from the language textbook, to fill in blanks on worksheets or workbook pages, or to read a story in the basal reader and answer questions, teachers can plan so that children learn and use language for real purposes that touch their lives directly. For example, children might be encouraged to choose to write friendly letters to real people, to fill out applications to join clubs—Arthur Fan Club and Reading Association (Little, Brown & Co.)—or to write business letters asking for free materials or inquiring about something they're studying in school. For reading, children need not be in a group, reading every story in a basal reader. Instead, they can read self-selected literature and then have conferences with their teacher or interact with a small group of peers about a book they have all read. Reading, especially trade books, and writing should be a part of all content areas and not limited to a specific time slot of the day.

This type of classroom is based on the following theory:

- Children construct their own knowledge from within rather than having it imposed on them from some outside source,

- Language arts are social activities and are best learned through interaction with others,

- Learning to read and write will emerge naturally as children engage in these processes in authentic ways using whole and real-life materials.

The curriculum known as whole language best describes a classroom where this theory is used as a framework for instructional practice. Whole language is described by Goodman et al. as "curricula that keep language whole and in the context of its thoughtful use in real situations." (9, p. 6).*

In the United States today, it is not easy for teachers to maintain classrooms that reflect current knowledge of how children develop as thinkers, readers, and writers. The emphasis on mastery learning and the movement "back to basics" have had a powerful impact on school curriculums. Schools and teachers are pressured to make sure that children master skills and perform well on achievement tests. Learning has become synonymous with achievement as measured by isolated bits and pieces of information on standardized tests. This, in turn, has led to a fragmented curriculum in which children spend most of their school day practicing skills that are isolated from meaningful context. Even kindergarteners are drilled on skills in a meaningless way in order to do well on standardized tests. Performance on tests has become the purpose of

---

*Numbers in parentheses appearing in the text refer to the Bibliography beginning on page 76.

schooling; schools vie for the "honor" of having the highest test scores.

Teachers have become managers of tests, worksheets, and children's activities. They try to keep up with the skills checklists as they document skills taught and "mastered" and as they plow through the tons of ditto paper and workbooks used to teach the skills. It is no wonder, then, that many have come to feel more and more like file clerks and bookkeepers rather than teachers.

Life in this kind of environment isn't pleasant for children either. Often, they do tasks that are meaningless to them in order to please the teacher or just to get through the day. School for many children, even in the primary grades, is a series of tests. The school year is often spent preparing for the state-mandated tests which, in some states, include a nationally standardized achievement test, a state minimum competency test, and a locally developed basic competency test.

Although school life isn't bleak for all children and teachers, there are too many "pressure cooker" classrooms in our schools where "learning" is pointless and teaching defies what is known about how children grow and develop as learners. When reading and writing are fragmented into atomistic pieces and isolated from broader contexts, children will not experience language as joyful, authentic, and natural. For the development of literacy to be enjoyable and natural, children have to engage in real, meaningful, and whole learning experiences. They need access to a wide variety of print materials and much time to personally interact with the materials. Pg. 58

There is not *a* set of blueprints for a whole-language classroom. Each teacher creates the curriculum in his/her classroom, based on his/her personal understanding of theory and research, his/her own goals and values, and his/her understanding of how children construct knowledge. Teachers who have been most effective in implementing a whole-language curriculum are those who hold in common the following convictions:

1. *Reading and writing should be a natural outgrowth of oral language development.* Most children begin school with well-developed oral language. They know a lot about language and how it works. Teachers ought to regard reading and writing as natural extensions of early language learning and focus on the language strengths children bring to school.

9

2. *Children construct their own knowledge from within.* Children use their prior knowledge and experience to construct new knowledge from reading, writing, and listening. Teachers, therefore, are obliged constantly to provide opportunities for children to draw upon their past experiences and to become more active agents in their own learning.

3. *Reading is comprehension*, that is, *creating meaning from text.* The focus of teaching had best be on how to help readers and writers attend to whole text, not merely to words, letters, and other bits and pieces of language. To do this, reading materials must be meaningful, predictable, and authentic.

4. *Communication is the main aim of writing.* To become good communicators in writing, children require much practice and encouragement. Teachers can encourage children to communicate what they know by letting them select their own writing topics, accepting their attempts to express themselves, and making certain they have an audience for sharing their writing.

5. *Learning to read and write is a social process.* An exchange of viewpoints contributes significantly to children's construction of knowledge; they think critically when they defend their own ideas and listen to other points of view. Therefore, it is incumbent upon teachers to arrange for children to interact with one another about their reading and writing.

6. *Risk taking and making mistakes are critical to reading and writing well.* Making errors is a natural part of learning as children go through various levels of being wrong. In this way, they construct their own coherent written language systems. Teachers have to encourage children to be autonomous and self-directed learners who aren't afraid of making mistakes.

In the chapters that follow, we explain in more detail the basis of these convictions and how they can provide the foundation for an approach to reading and writing that is truly natural and enjoyable for children.

10

Chapter 1
LANGUAGE ARTS AND THE CONSTRUCTION OF KNOWLEDGE

Reading and writing are processes central to all areas of the curriculum. It is important, therefore, that teachers develop a curriculum that supports the natural literacy evolution of young children. To do so, it's necessary to understand how children develop as readers and writers and to be aware that children construct knowledge about written language in the same way they form knowledge about the world. A teacher who realizes that children construct their own knowledge will not blindly follow commercial materials or use learning activities that may be meaningless to them.

Teachers with an understanding of how children develop literacy will not expect them to read exactly what is on a page in a book for they know that reading is a process in which children create meaning from print and in doing so they do not always read with 100 percent accuracy. They know that young children invent their spelling at an early stage of spelling development and that to insist on correct spelling when they compose stories may undermine their efforts to figure out the spelling system. They also know that children create their own hypotheses about how reading and writing work and they observe carefully as new hypotheses are developed.

One of the most important skills of a primary teacher is to be a good child watcher, which means to sensitively observe a child's thinking and literacy development. For instance, the teacher notices how children create meaning from text, how they invent spelling, how their vocabularies develop, and how they construct relationships. Teachers then can encourage children to make relationships between what they already know and new information and can help them explore meaning as they read or write. Teachers will use practices appropriate for the child based on the knowledge they have gained as child watchers along with their understanding of the reading and writing processes.

Primary teachers will find it helpful to convey to children that they enjoy and value reading and writing and they need to assure that children see them engaged in these processes. The teacher and children are a community of readers and writers; they support one another and share their reading and writing. In such a classroom, one would see teachers and children reading and writing about a variety of subjects. Examples of children's individual and group writing would be displayed. A variety of literature would be available: magazines, books, picture books, wordless books, big books, reference books, and poetry books. The materials of all genres would be in bookcases, on walls, on chart racks, on tables, on window sills, and in writing folders—all easily accessible to the children.

It is advantageous to have a reading area that is comfortable for children. In some classrooms with wall-to-wall children, there is no space available either for a reading loft or an area rug with pillows; however, space sometimes can be found for a few carpet squares in a corner. Because classrooms vary so much, there is no single design but it is important that teachers try to create a comfortable and inviting space where children can go to read.

Teachers will find it useful also to help parents understand how children develop literacy. Most parents, who have already helped their children develop as oral language users, want to do what is best for their children but they do not always know what to do. Together, teachers, administrators, and parents can develop parent education programs that inform parents about the value of reading aloud to their children, taking them to the library, and providing as many experiences as the family can afford. It is also important to inform parents about how to help children with appropriate homework.

THE PRIMARY LITERACY PROGRAM

Children's literature should be the backbone of any reading program. It's essential that teachers read to children every day. Many teachers start the school day with a short picture book and later in the day, often after lunch, read from a longer book. During the year, they read from a variety of genres so children can become acquainted with all types of literature. There is also a time during each day for children to read silently from self-selected books.

Books chosen for children should be in language that is natural and not contrived to control vocabulary or to conform to the skills to be learned. Most reading texts for young children are designated for a specific grade level and do not take into account individual children's prior knowledge, interest, or purpose for reading. Texts such as basal readers designed for beginners often are uninteresting, make use of words that follow certain patterns, have short, choppy sentences, and frequently lack coherence. The writing style usually makes it difficult for young children to make predictions about the story, and often the text does not sound like natural language.

It is desirable that all reading and writing activities be authentic and meaningful to the children. Books should be good literature. Writing should be purposeful; thank-you notes, get-well cards, and letters to friends and relatives are examples of authentic writing experiences.

A whole-language program had best emphasize children's interests. Children come to school with varied interests, which may or may not be those of the teacher or the formal curriculum. Since children have to have something to read and write about, it is expedient to use something that is of interest to them as a guide in the selection of books and writing topics. This is important for the following reasons:

1. When children are interested in something, they will care enough about it to grapple with it and search for meaning. If it is a subject they don't care about, they are less likely to put forth effort in trying to construct meaning.

2. When children write, their best topics are usually those that are personal to them. They will write more easily, if they are allowed to choose their own topics.

LANGUAGE ARTS—AN INTEGRAL PART OF THE TOTAL SCHOOL DAY

In many of our schools today, the curriculum has been fragmented into artificial and meaningless parts. This is especially true in the language arts. Reading, writing, listening, and speaking have no predetermined content; their content may come from areas of science, social studies, math, literature, and the child's world.

Language Arts and the Construction of Knowledge (see Figure 1-1) suggests how children think and construct knowledge and the central role that literacy plays in the process. Children bring prior knowledge and differing amounts of interest to any topic of study. The model is not meant to suggest sequential steps, since thinking occurs as a whole and in many different ways. The language arts are an integral part of the model because listening and reading are two important sources for information, and speaking, writing, and drama are processes by which we construct and express meaning. The following discussion describes activities consistent with this model.

Selection of Topic

A topic for study in the classroom is more meaningful when it can grow out of the interests of the learners. But, whether the topic is selected by the teacher or the children, the content need not be limited to subject areas. For example, in studying the topic of insects, children might want to study different kinds of insects, their habits and life cycle, the balance of nature, and ecological issues. Children might want to examine the size of insects, and count and classify them, or they might want to study climate and insects, geographical areas of certain insects, and how insects affect agriculture. In the beginning of the study of a topic, the content cannot be fully determined because the children's interests and the availability of resources may either expand or restrict the study.

Use of Information Sources

At the beginning of any study, it is important to acknowledge that children already have some prior knowledge about the topic. Some, of course, have more fully developed ideas than others and this will affect their construction of new knowledge. It is especially important for a teacher to find out what children already know and one way to do this is to ask them. Let's take insects again as an example.

When asked what they knew, children in one group of second graders said, "Some insects sting," "There are some that buzz," "Bees and wasps live in hives or something like that." One child said, "I know that flies like to eat blood," and another said, "I can't think of any good reason to have insects but there probably is one."

Figure 1-1. Language Arts and the Construction of Knowledge.

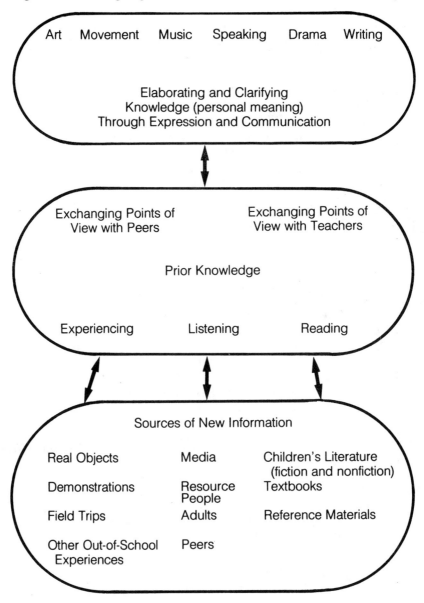

When asked how they could find out more about insects, this group of second graders decided on three ways they wanted to get more information. Some said, "I'd like to read about them in different books." Others said, "Go outside and look at insects," and others said, "Get some filmstrips and tapes and other things like that from the library."

The cognitive level of children, their reading abilities, and available resources are factors that need to be taken into account when children and the teacher consider and select ways to gain information. It is especially important for children to have hands-on experiences as well as to listen and read about a topic. When possible, teachers might use real objects that can be touched, smelled, heard, seen, and sometimes tasted; they also might arrange to have classroom demonstrations by resource people and field trips to places such as a museum of natural history or a zoo. Responding to the children's request to read, a teacher will make available children's literature, nonfiction and fiction, as well as textbooks and reference materials.

ROLE OF THE TEACHER AND PEERS
IN CHILDREN'S CONSTRUCTION OF KNOWLEDGE

Through social interaction, children exchange points of view and in this way they help one another as they construct new knowledge. A child who believes that a caterpillar cannot turn into a butterfly may begin to question that belief if enough classmates tell about seeing cocoons and what happened as they observed the life cycles of butterflies and other insects, or the child may request more tangible evidence from peers.

The teacher also assists in the process of knowledge construction. Sometimes she or he asks questions that cause a child to reflect on relationships between his/her prior knowledge and the new information. She or he might purposefully present information that is in conflict with information some children are likely to have, causing them to rethink or support their own point of view. For example, playing devil's advocate and suggesting that instead of a butterfly, a grasshopper might come out of the cocoon may remind a child of a discussion the class had following a filmstrip in which they learned that a little grasshopper looks like the adult. Other children might give other evidence and then someone may decide to check in a reference book to show that the life cycle of a butterfly is different from that of a grasshopper.

SELECTION OF MODES FOR EXPRESSION OF IDEAS

Just as children like to find out about different things in different ways, they also have preferences about how they express their thinking. In the second-grade classroom mentioned above, when asked how they would like to let others know about the results of their research, some said, "I want to do an oral report." Other children wanted to draw insects. One group wanted to write reports and one group said, "We want to sing and make different voices and act like different insects."

When children express themselves through writing, speaking, drama, music, art, and movement, they clarify for themselves what they know as they select ways to represent their thoughts. These expressions allow teachers to observe children's thinking.

With the model in mind, teachers are urged to consider the reading and writing practices suggested in the next two chapters and decide which ones they prefer to introduce in their classrooms. Of course, the more autonomous teachers are, the freer they are to test out numerous practices in the classroom.

Chapter 2
PRACTICES FOR DEVELOPING LITERACY: READING

Reading and writing are communication processes. For discussion purposes, we have given our ideas and suggestions about these processes in separate chapters, realizing that practices overlap and that reading and writing are indivisible. We realize too that what may be appropriate for one group of kindergarteners may be used with a group of second graders as well. For this reason, we were reluctant to assign suggested grade levels, even though some suggestions are primarily for beginning readers and writers and others are for more proficient written-language users. For example, big books are generally associated with kindergarten and first-grade programs, but they can be used with older children as well. Also, dictated stories and labeling of pictures are usually not done beyond first grade, but there may be some in second and third grade who would benefit from these activities.

Descriptions of the practices recommended for reading and writing are brief. However, we included enough information so that you could implement them in your classroom. Needless to say, we have not included every whole-language practice. The Annotated Bibliography (pp. 78-80) includes sources that provide more information. You will notice that many of these practices are not new; however, all are within the framework of a whole-language program.

READING ALOUD TO CHILDREN

Reading aloud daily from good children's literature continues to be an important practice for teachers of young children. Fortunately, this practice has withstood the passage of time, but we continue to hear of many teachers who think they don't have the time to do this. Reading aloud is an essential element of a whole-language program.

Children enjoy having books read to them. The wonderful trade books now available, particularly picture books, charm children with their delightful characters, warm and often humorous plots, and the aesthetics of the illustrations. For many, it is their first experience of being read to and of hearing the beautiful sound of language from books. In addition to the pleasure derived, children also learn about starting at the front of a book, turning pages, noticing characteristics of print, and realizing that the print conveys meaning.

As children create meaning from a text by making relationships between their prior knowledge and the text, they develop new knowlege. When children listen to *The Grouchy Ladybug* (4), they use their knowledge of insects, time, size relationships, and different emotions to understand the story. Additionally, they build new knowledge about ladybugs, and most young children are fascinated by them. A fun book to read after *The Grouchy Ladybug* is *I Love Ladybugs* (2).

Most primary teachers already know about the value of reading aloud to children and do so as a regular part of the school day. Some teachers begin the day with a book, others use a book following a play activity or before a quiet activity. There is no magic formula for when or how to read aloud but it's important that teachers show enthusiasm and get children involved in the story. They may have children predict what's going to happen next, discuss a part of the story, or give an oral response to predictable words or phrases in the story. Children should hear all genres of children's literature, literature of different cultures, and literature written in different dialects. They should become acquainted with a variety of books and authors. Included in this publication is a list of some of our favorites (Appendix A); you will have others to add.

In addition to reading aloud to children for enjoyment, teachers use many books that relate to content being studied in the classroom. For example, there are books related to units of study about trains, buses, airplanes, and boats that can be used when studying transportation. There are children's books available that are related to all subject areas that might be studied.

You can help to increase children's understanding of a book by asking them to predict what they think will happen next. After hearing a book read aloud, it is useful to ask them to make connections between what they know and the content of the book. Occasionally, teachers are overzealous in their attempts to question children; it is also appropriate just to ask them what they liked or thought about as they listened.

ORAL READING

Oral reading has long been a tradition in elementary schools, but it usually consists of one child after another reading a paragraph or page from the basal reader. This type of oral reading is referred to as "round-robin" reading, which we believe has little or no value in improving a child's ability to read. In this situation, there is usually not even an "audience" as the teacher is busy making sure all are keeping their eyes on the page or playing "catch me if you can" (listening for mistakes of the reader in order to correct them immediately). The other children are frantically trying to look ahead so they will know which part they're going to read. Most children do like to read aloud, but oral reading should have a purpose other than just to read aloud for the sake of reading aloud.

There are many opportunities for purposeful oral reading in the classroom. Following the silent reading of a story, children can be asked questions and to support their answer by reading from the text. They might read passages they found to be humorous or sad, their favorite part, or the part where they knew how the story was going to end. They could read dialogue with the same expression they think the character in the story used.

Reading plays is an especially good activity for oral reading as children practice becoming a character in the play. Peers can help each other decide how the characters would say their parts. Children's expression will be improved and their understanding of characterization deepened as they read different roles.

Many teachers use choral reading for improving oral interpretation, often starting with the entire class reading simultaneously. Later, more complex forms of choral reading are introduced where individuals or groups read specified parts. This activity is popular with children and choral readings are readily accessible to teachers as they can be found in numerous publications.

Perhaps the major value of oral reading occurs when teachers listen to individual children read aloud and assess how the child is processing print. Listening to a child read orally and noting his/her miscues (something said that is different from the text) is one of the best ways to know how the child is thinking as he/she reads. When teachers listen with a "miscue ear," they learn how the child is thinking as he or she reads and can plan strategy lessons to help him or her become a more proficient reader. This process, known as miscue analysis, is further discussed in the assessment section. (For a more in-depth description of miscue analysis, see Goodman, Watson, and Burke [11]).

LANGUAGE FOR ENJOYMENT

Teachers of young children have wonderful opportunities to make language learning fun. There are lots of materials and activities for finger plays, choral reading, and poetry sharing (see Appendix B for a list of some of our favorites). Records and tapes are available. Many poems have been set to music; teachers and children can compose their own. Movement and drama are excellent ways to enjoy communication.

Imagine this scene: The children are acting out pecking movements with their heads, dramatizing rain and lightning with their fingers and arms, and making thunder by clapping their hands as they recite "The Woodpecker" by Elizabeth Madox Roberts (20). Many teachers are familiar with this delightful poem which proved to be such fun for children in Mrs. Hicks' kindergarten class.

Such activities are valuable for language development. Have you seen a child smile when "Five little pumpkins sitting on a fence, one fell off ..." or other seasonal and general poems or other language forms are sung or recited? In addition to enjoying the activity and building positive attitudes for future language learning, there are other benefits. Singing and reciting different poems and songs help children extend their oral communication abilities. Their vocabulary is increased as they learn new words and create meaning for those words through enjoyable activities. Children learn about different forms of language as they gain experience with a variety of written text.

USING BIG BOOKS

A big book is simply an enlargement of a regular book and many teachers use them as an integral part of their reading program. Children learn much about reading as they read with a group of classmates from a big book. Big books of songs, poems, and jingles are available also. They can be purchased commercially (see Appendix C for a list of publishers), or teachers can make their own, using poster board or other similar material, copying the artwork from favorite picture books onto the poster board, and writing the print in much the same way you see it in the book. Some teachers use an opaque projector to help them construct big books.

Let's visit a classroom. Mrs. Hicks, a kindergarten teacher, has placed a big book on an easel and stands ready with her finger or pointer. The first time through the book she reads the text, pointing to the words as she reads. She is careful to read the whole text naturally and does not dwell on individual words or sentences.

What is happening as she reads this big book, even the first time? First of all, it is enjoyable for the children. And, because she is reading the book normally, the children are learning many literary and linguistic factors. In *The Foundations of Literacy*, Holdaway (15) describes these linguistic factors as: the syntax of language, vocabulary development (by hearing words not used in their normal conversation), intonation patterns, in which children hear new literacy patterns that vary from conversation, and idioms that use special forms different from normal grammatical or syntactic rules.

Additionally, the child is learning left to right progression, how books are organized, story structure, and much more. Most kindergarteners and some first graders are not looking specifically at the words or letters but by reading big books they will eventually construct the relationship between the print and the meaning of the text.

Now back to the classroom. Following the first reading of the story, the teacher repeats the reading and the children join in with her as they are able. She continues to use the big book over and over on other days until the story is familiar to all of the children. The teacher, at a later time, may want to focus on some individual words by asking, "Can you tell where it says "Happy birthday," or "Can you tell me which part you are finding difficult?" In this way, she may focus attention on parts of language but this is always done within the context of the story.

We feel strongly about the value of big books; they help to develop readers. Everyone in the class works together to read the big book. There are no blue birds chirping their advanced tune or dumb birds tracing letters. All children are readers, even though they may be at different levels of literacy development, and they read in a natural and enjoyable setting that involves everyone. Moreover, instead of focusing on isolated words and letters, they read words in the context of an entire story.

In many classrooms, the experience with the big book is followed by reading small copies of the book individually or in pairs. Because the books they are reading are predictable and familiar, the children experience success.

Many teachers follow the reading of a big book such as *In a Dark Dark Wood* (18) by writing parallel stories based on the patterns in the text of the familiar story (see Figure 2-1). Children learn story structure and have a sense of creating their own meaning in print when they write parallel stories.

Figure 2-1. A parallel story.

ORIGINAL STORY	PARALLEL STORY
In a Dark Dark Wood,* a traditional rhyme collected by June Melser and Joy Cowley	*In a Dark Dark Neighborhood*, a parallel story by Mrs. Bagby and her kindergarten class
In a dark dark wood,	In a dark dark neighborhood,
There was a dark dark path.	There was a dark dark street.
And up that dark dark path	And up that dark dark street,
There was a dark dark house.	There was a dark dark park.
And in that dark dark house,	And in that dark dark park,
There was a dark dark stair.	There was a dark dark sidewalk.
And up that dark dark stair,	And up that dark dark sidewalk,
There was a dark dark room.	There was a dark dark playhouse.
And in that dark dark room,	And in that dark dark playhouse,
There was a dark dark cupboard.	There was a dark dark hall.
And in that dark dark cupboard,	And down that dark dark hall,
There was a dark dark box.	There was a dark dark room.
And in that dark dark box,	And in that dark dark room,
There was a	There was a
GHOST!	BIRTHDAY PARTY!

**In a Dark Dark Wood* is part of The Story Box Collection, available from the following publisher: The Wright Group, 10949 Technology Place, San Diego, CA 92127.

Big books play a significant part in a beginning reading program and it is advisable that kindergarten and first-grade teachers use them on a daily basis. In addition, they can be used by children on their own, either individually or in pairs.

SINGING

Children usually enter school with a repertoire of songs they have learned to sing at home or in preschool. These known songs and new ones are useful for reading development. Singing is fun and enjoyable for most children. An old familiar song enjoyed in Mrs. Hamrick's second-grade classroom is "This Old Man" which, as you probably know, goes like this:

This old man, he played one,
He played knick-knack on my thumb,
With a knick-knack, paddy-whack
Give your dog a bone,
This old man came rolling home.

Mrs. Hamrick sometimes uses transparencies and an overhead projector to project the words of a song on a screen so all of the children can see the words and sing along. This song—like most—can be rewritten like you would a parallel story by changing man, the numbers, the body parts, and the dog. Mrs. Hamrick sometimes uses the transparency text like a big book and points to the text while she and the children sing the song. In using singing as a regular part of her literacy program, Mrs. Hamrick fosters enjoyment of written text.

GROUP READING

Have you seen Bill Martin (*Brown Bear, Brown Bear*—see Appendix A) distribute books to a group of children? It is a most inspirational experience. After he distributes books, he asks groups of three children to read the book. Each group sits on the floor around a book and together they figure out the words and story. What one doesn't know, the others seem to know. After struggling and often arguing over words, they make it through the book. Then children start at the beginning and read the book. Everyone is part of the group and all feel pride in their accomplishment. Observing Bill Martin's process reveals the value of children working together to read a text. You can observe the thinking and cooperation occurring in each group.

COOKING

Cooking is an important part of a language arts curriculum and many primary teachers are aware of its value. Cooking is fun and helps children to see a reason for reading. For example, you read recipes to know how to make things to eat. In addition, cooking is one way of extending books. For instance, Miss Waldrup, a kindergarten teacher, follows the reading aloud of one of Milne's *Winnie the Pooh* books with a "Bear's Delight." The recipe includes 1/2 cup of honey, 1/2 cup of butter or margarine, ground cinnamon, and crackers or bread. Measure the ingredients, mix the honey with the softened butter, spread the mixture on crackers or bread, and sprinkle the top with cinnamon. The implements you will need are a mixing bowl, a measuring cup, a spoon for stirring, and a knife for spreading.

It's a delight to see Miss Waldrup and her children as they savor the food they make and extend the enjoyment of favorite books. She says children benefit from such cooking activities in several ways: enjoyment, social interaction, following directions, and working cooperatively, to name just a few. There are many children's books in which food is a part of the story, and the perfect way to make the books memorable and alive is to extend them with a cooking activity (see Appendix D for a list of some of our favorites).

HEARING TEXT, THEN READING

While this may sound like a shocking suggestion to some, many teachers realize the value of children hearing stories before they read them for the first time. Suzanne Stringer, a first-grade teacher, reads stories aloud to children before they read the stories themselves. In this way, children become familiar with the story and are much more likely to succeed in reading it independently. She finds that children are eager to read independently those stories they enjoyed hearing.

RECORDED READ-ALONGS

Children enjoy listening to literature read aloud and they also enjoy reading along with a reader on a tape or record. Beeping signals help the child know when to turn a page. Numerous books with accompanying tapes or records are available commercially or can be made by having someone read aloud into a tape recorder. Parent volunteers, older children, or the teacher can make the tapes; children like hearing familiar voices on tape. The tapes and books are used by individual children or by a group of children at a listening center. The reasons for listening to a tape and reading along with a book are similar to those for assisted reading or being read to by someone: When children see print as they listen to the story, it may help them to make the needed connections; when they hear a story read over and over, they gain an understanding of it and an ability to predict what it's about. As they continue to listen and read along, their predictions are either confirmed or rejected. They feel the power of being a reader when they can later read the story alone.

ASSISTED READING

Assisted reading is sometimes referred to as echo reading. A good reader, such as a teacher, parent volunteer, older child, or peer, reads a text aloud and at the same time a child who is struggling with reading follows along, reading aloud also. The reader can be seated on an adult's lap or next to the proficient reader. The reading can be repeated as many times as the reader cares to follow along. Assisted reading can be followed by having the less proficient reader read the text independently. The independent reading isn't always necessary, especially if the child doesn't wish to do so.

READING INDEPENDENTLY

There are many different ways to have children read independently in the classroom. One of the most popular ones has been sustained silent reading (SSR), in which a teacher sets aside a certain time for everyone to read self-selected books. Usually a longer time is alloted for more proficient readers.

Many teachers give time for children to read self-selected books, but only after they have finished all of their other work. For some children, especially the weaker readers, this time never comes because they don't finish their assigned work. Giving time for all children to read independently is important for several reasons. Beginning readers can benefit by looking at pictures in picture books and wordless books. They can also "read" books that have been read aloud to them over and over. The reluctant reader may begin to see reading as a pleasurable leisure time activity during a time set aside for independent reading. All children need practice in reading and time in the classroom will give them this opportunity.

Teachers need some system to record what children are reading. Usually a card for each child where the names of the books are listed along with dates is sufficient. Some teachers add a line telling whether or not the child liked the book or some other brief comments made by the child.

Often teachers are expected to assign homework; independent reading of self-selected books is a good homework assignment. Asking children to write lengthy reports or to analyze characters often detracts from the enjoyment of reading and usually has a negative effect on the child's interest in reading. This does not mean that children shouldn't discuss books they read or do some limited writing about them, but with young children in particular such activities should be limited or voluntary so that the enjoyment of reading is not affected negatively.

READING CONFERENCES

One of our favorite practices for promoting growth in reading is the individual reading conference (17). After a child has started reading a self-selected book, the child and the teacher have a conference about the book. Let's sit in on a conference that Ann Dominick, a third-grade teacher, conducted with Anna. Anna arrived for her reading conference and sat close to Ms. Dominick (T is Ms. Dominick and A is Anna).

T: Hi, Anna. What did you bring to read today? Oh, that's right, *Beezus and Ramona*.
A: Yes, and I finished the whole book.
T: You passed your goal, then?
A: I said I was going to read to page 99, but I couldn't stop reading. It was so

27

good and so funny.

T: That's great! What part of the book have you chosen to read to me today?

A: The part where Beezus gets to take art lessons from Miss Robbins.

At this point, Anna read the page that told about the dragon Beezus painted. At one point in the text, Ms. Robbins said, "Here's a girl with real imagination. . . . Beezus smiled modestly at her toes while the mothers admired her picture. . . ." When Anna read this section, the teacher noticed that Anna pronounced modestly, "mostly."

T: Let me ask you about this last sentence. How do you think Beezus would have smiled when she was looking down at the coat?

A: Kinda like embarrassed.

T: And do you know what this word is? (pointing at the word, modestly in the text).

A: Probably embarrassed or something like that.

T: It is a little like embarrassed. Can you think of a word that begins with an "m" that would make sense here?

A: (No response from Anna.)

T: Have you ever heard the word, modest? Oh, they are just being modest. (Ms. Dominick reads the sentence from the book.) It is like being a little embarrassed because everyone was saying how good she was. Can you read the sentence now?

A: Beezus smiled modestly. . . .

T: Can you think of a time when you've been modest?

A: Oh, you see there was this time that my mama made a dress for me and I wore it on Sunday and everybody said, "Oh, you look so cute in that." I was kinda embarrassed, but I was happy, too.

T: So you were modest then. It's like when you don't admit you look nice even if you know you do look good.

T: Can you tell me how the book ends?

A: Beezus gets real mad at herself because she doesn't like her sister.

T: Is Beezus angry with Ramona?

A: Oh, she just doesn't like her sister.

T: Well, I have the same problem with my brother. He's always making a mess and getting into my things.

T: Is that why Beezus says she doesn't like Ramona?

A: Yes.

T: Do you think Beezus will learn to like her sister?

A: Maybe as she gets older she won't make such a big mess.

T: Now that you have finished *Beezus and Ramona*, what book do you plan to read next?

A: Oh, I'm going to pick another Cleary book.

T: You must really like Beverly Cleary.

A: I love her books.

We chose this conference between Ms. Dominick and Anna because the teacher is an experienced child watcher. She knows the benefits of having individual conferences with children and is a skillful questioner. She listened carefully to Anna's thinking as she read and used a "teachable moment" to work with Anna when she miscued on the word, modestly. Anna related the story to a situation in her own life and suggested its resolution.

During a reading conference, a teacher has a number of options. For instance, she/he can have a child read to her/him, retell a story, or respond to questions. In addition, she/he can have a child talk about a reading selection, and she/he can assess what sense the child is making of the text.

STRATEGY LESSONS

When children experience difficulty with reading text, a teacher has to determine the cause of the problem. Why is the child not constructing meaning when he/she reads? Is it a lack of prior knowledge, the language structure, a lack of sound-symbol relationships, or a combination of problems? Through an analysis of a child's miscues, the teacher can determine what is interfering with the child creating meaning from text. Once the problem or problems are determined, the teacher can plan strategy lessons to assist the reader in creating meaning based on the same type of text (fiction or nonfiction) with which the child is experiencing difficulty.

Goodman and Burke's *Reading Strategies: Focus on Comprehension* (10) has examples of strategy lessons that teachers can use or modify for children in their classrooms. Their suggested strategies are always in the context of meaning and the emphasis is on process rather than on product. (Conversely, a skills approach is product oriented, the goal being to get right answers. The teacher usually dominates the skills lesson. If children have difficulty, they are given more time and more work on the particular skill difficulty.)

An example from the Goodman and Burke book (10) is designed to help readers distinguish between fiction and nonfiction text by examining cues a reader receives from the title or table of contents, previous experience with the author, and the language of the material. Goodman and Burke use Kipling's, "How the Whale Got His Throat," and a description about whales from an encyclopedia, entitled, "Whales." First, readers are asked to state which title sounds like fiction or nonfiction. Since young readers would have little, if any, experience reading Kipling, they probably could not make a judgment by considering the type of text the author usually writes. If they were shown the book that contained Kipling's work and a copy of the encyclopedia, third graders can classify them as fiction or nonfiction based on what they know about encyclopedias and books with collections of stories and thus predict the type of text. This information orients the reader's expectations as he or she starts to read.

Goodman and Burke (10) also include a strategy lesson that helps the reader develop meaning through context if the word in the text is unfamiliar. The strategy helps the reader confirm the meaning of the word in several ways. The reader first decides if knowing the word is necessary in order to make sense of the text. If not, the reader continues reading. If the reader decides it is necessary, then the teacher encourages the child to predict what the word is, based on everything learned in the story and the reader's prior knowledge. Each time a child comes up with a possible word, the teacher asks if the word makes sense in the context of the sentence. If it doesn't make sense, she/he encourages the child to continue searching for a word that does make sense.

A teacher can develop a strategy lesson that helps students predict, confirm, and integrate content with prior knowledge. Teachers can use books, poems, or other whole texts such as newspaper clippings and comic strips, or they can write their own text for a needed strategy. An example of a strategy lesson to practice prediction is based on the book *Sylvester and the Magic Pebble* (22). The teacher reads the book in parts, stopping to ask children to predict the emotions and behaviors of Sylvester and his parents. Good stopping places are when the lion approaches Sylvester, when Sylvester doesn't come home, and when his parents go on a picnic. Children make their various predictions and as the teacher continues to read they compare their predictions with the way the author developed the character.

A strategy lesson that could be used for predicting character elements is based on the story *Frederick* (16). The teacher reads the first part of the book where all of the mice are gathering food to store for the winter in the stone wall. Everyone, that is, except Frederick. Since Frederick didn't help gather food, what do the children think Frederick would contribute to the long winter in the stone wall? After the children offer different predictions, the teacher continues reading. Even though all the predictions are legitimate, only those who predicted what Frederick did could confirm their predictions. Some children will find that their meanings were different from the text.

These strategy lessons are useful for children who are progressing as readers, and they are also helpful for those who are focused on sounding out words correctly rather than on meaning. Strategy lessons are recommended as far more meaningful activities than the traditional instruction outlined in most basal manuals. Teachers can use and adapt lessons developed by Goodman and Burke (10), or develop their own. The lessons can be used with individual readers, small groups, or in some cases with an entire class of children.

READING THE SAME BOOK

A successful practice to use as an alternative to a traditional reading group consists of having a group of children choose to read the same book. You need enough copies of the book for every child in the group. The set of books should be quality literature as well as appealing to the particular group.

Sharon Tanory, a third-grade teacher, recently had a small group of children who selected White's, *Charlotte's Web* (24). Although several in the group had heard the book read orally, they had not read it themselves. They read a chapter each day and discussed it. In the beginning, several said they knew the story well. After reading and discussing a few chapters, they realized there were different interpretations for passages and that each child created a slightly different meaning. *Charlotte's Web* became increasingly enjoyable for the children as they constructed meaning about the book for themselves. They later chose to read White's other books: *The Trumpet of the Swan* (26) and *Stuart Little* (25). Throughout the reading and discussion of the books, children pursued several activities: exploration of encyclopedias and nonfiction books on mice, spiders, pigs, and swans; development of spontaneous and planned creative dramatic presentations; reports about the characters; and artistic representations of scenes.

...ᴄᴇ is appropriate at any grade level; we've seen it used ...ᴄᴄssfully even with first graders. The only criteria are that children want to and can read the book they select (see Appendix E for a list of predictable books). When children read the same book together, they learn from each other by listening and responding to each other's points of view. Enthusiasm for reading increases as they enjoy literature together.

CLOZE PROCEDURE

The reader of this publication may get the impression that we are against all paper and pencil activities; however, we only oppose worksheets and workbooks that are not whole language. One type of worksheet we do support is the cloze procedure, in which individual words are deleted from meaningful text and children are asked to supply the missing words. Here the emphasis is on getting children to select words that make sense to them and at the same time keep the intended meaning of the author. It's best if children work on cloze activities in pairs or small groups because they will benefit from the interaction with each other. In *Cloze Procedure and the Teaching of Reading*, Rye (21) provides a comprehensive review of the cloze procedure as a testing and teaching device.

COMPUTERS AND READING

All children don't need to be "plugged" to computers for a certain number of minutes per day or week to do exercises that look just like the page of a workbook. At the same time, computers may be of value to children if appropriate software programs are used. However, computer time must not replace the reading of children's quality literature.

There is good software and bad software; judging its value depends on your perception of how children develop as readers. We judge software as inferior if it focuses on skills in which there is no real text. The market is inundated with software fitting this description that is no better than ditto sheets and workbook pages that usually focus only on specific skills isolated from meaningful text. With this kind of software, the computer becomes simply an electronic workbook.

32

However, there is software that can be useful. Cloze or maze activities using meaningful text in which readers select words that make sense help children to predict and confirm in reading. There are also short stories with comprehension questions that may interest some readers. Interactive story types of software in which children select different characters, settings, and endings for stories may help improve children's reading. We think word-processing programs have value to children; they can create their own text and get a copy instantly to revise and share. There are software programs described as language experience; some of these are good, but others narrowly control the vocabulary of the child and make the lesson no better than a typical lesson in a basal reader.

TRANSFORMATION OF PUBLISHED READING PROGRAMS

Some teachers are required to use the school's adopted basal reader series. If you are required to use such a program, we hope you are at least given some freedom to adapt it to your own situation and to the interests and development of your children. Some teachers have the children read the stories in the basal reader on a self-selected basis and may confer or discuss the story with them in an individual conference. If several children have read the story, they can get together to discuss it; the discussion may be child- or teacher-directed. If you are required to use the activities suggested in the manual, use those suggestions at the end of each lesson that are usually labeled "enrichment." These suggestions are usually more meaning centered and thus will help children focus on meaning as they read. If workbooks or worksheets are required, carefully select those pages that are most meaningful rather than having children do all of them. And when children complete the exercises, encourage them to work together in pairs or small groups to discuss and compare their responses. Instead of correcting the worksheets, ask children to justify or explain their answers. Do not focus on one correct answer. Children doing the same exercise could negotiate their choices and vote on the one or ones they think are correct. After several discussions you are likely to find that for most of the items on a worksheet or workbook page you could have several possible answers, some of which may be better than the ones provided by the publisher.

If you are required to use a basal reader and to conduct lessons with it, keep the lessons short and try not to have them every day. Remember that basal materials do not and should not make up your total reading program. It is best to have the focus of the program be on the reading of meaningful and interesting text. If you are not already doing so, we encourage you to try some of the practices we have suggested. They should make classroom reading more interesting for the children and more meaningful for you.

ASSESSING DEVELOPMENT OF READERS

To determine how children are developing as readers, a teacher has to observe how they are processing print as they read. One way to do this is to ask a child to read a text (whole text with a beginning and an end that is in the child's experience range) and then to ask him or her to retell the story. We recommend the unaided and aided retelling procedure suggested by Goodman, Watson, Burke (11), in which the teacher asks the child to tell the story and follows the retelling with more specific questions about what he or she has already related about the story. If the reader retells the text with most of its meaning, the teacher can assume the child understands the story. The unaided and aided retelling can be used as early as the child is able to read.

Miscue analysis is another assessment procedure that is most helpful (11). When assessing readers with difficulties, we encourage teachers to use the complete procedures outlined in the *Reading Miscue Inventory* (11). However, in most instances with typical readers, we simply note miscues children make as they read orally to us, and ask ourselves this question: Does the sentence make sense with the miscue? If it does, we judge the reader to be focused on meaning and we do not become concerned, realizing that all readers make these kinds of miscues.

The cloze procedure also is useful in determining whether a child is comprehending what he is reading. The teacher observes a child's ability to replace the deleted words with words that retain the basic meaning of the text (see page 32).

Keeping a record of the reading completed by a child is another helpful way to assess a child's reading growth. The child and teacher keep a list of books and stories that the child has read. Brief anecdotal comments may be included on the record.

When a teacher child watches, she or he makes significant observations about the child's reading habits, and finds answers to important assessment questions: Does the child choose reading from among different choices in the classroom? Is the child reluctant or enthusiastic when there are opportunities to select books from the classroom or central library? Will the child share information about what is being read? In shared literature experiences, does the child participate?

We are especially opposed to relying heavily on formal assessment procedures to judge a child's reading ability, particularly those procedures that purport to measure a child's reading isolated from meaningful text. Most standardized and criterion-referenced tests use only word parts, words in isolation, single sentences or short paragraphs to assess a child's reading ability. This type of evaluation reflects a belief that reading consists of isolated bits and pieces, and ignores the point that reading is a process of creating meaning from written text.

Reading tests built on a segmental view of reading do not measure real reading. Therefore, we suggest using the informal methods discussed in this section. In addition, some published informal reading inventories can be helpful if they focus on assessing children's comprehension of whole pieces of text rather than merely counting the number of oral reading errors the child makes. Finally, it is important that teachers keep a folder for each child that contains meaningful information. In this way, each child's reading growth can be documented and the record can be used as a basis for planning appropriate learning activities.

Chapter 3
PRACTICES FOR DEVELOPING LITERACY: WRITING

It is important that all children, including kindergarteners, begin writing the first week of school. The writing of most children in kindergarten and many in first grade will consist of pictures or strings of letters. Others will invent spelling, reflecting their understanding of sound-symbol correspondence.

Teachers should allocate time every day for children to write on self-selected topics. In classrooms where we work, teachers usually allot at least 30 to 40 minutes a day for writing. Following Graves's (12) suggestions, teachers spend a few minutes of the time writing themselves so that children can see them writing and then they conduct writing conferences with individual children (usually about one-fifth of the class each day). In addition to the individual formal conferences, teachers spend a few minutes interacting informally with other children as needed. At the end of the writing time, several children volunteer to read their writing to the class. All the children's writing pieces are kept in the room in individual writing folders.

A second-grade teacher, Linda Gurosky, tries to have each child publish one writing piece per month. That is, a child revises and polishes a self-selected story and puts it into book form or displays it on the wall. In Linda's classroom, writing time occurs daily. In addition, children write in their own personal journals each day for about 10 minutes. And, of course, she uses writing activities throughout the day as children write poems, keep learning logs in various subjects, do research reports, and participate in other meaningful writing activities.

The way teachers carry out their writing program depends on the developmental level of the children. For example, most kindergarteners would not revise or be expected to publish formal and polished pieces. Most kindergarten teachers we know, like Becky Davidson, simply have children write on large sheets of unlined paper and then keep these in a folder or notebook for each child. Hipple (14) provides several good ideas about writing in kindergarten and Calkins (3) gives us insights about kindergarten children's early forays into writing. Calkins reminds us to give children functional reasons for writing such as letter writing, taking messages, attendance taking, registering a vote for a pet's name, and making lists. It's important that teachers give children many opportunities and ample time to write, and receive their writing with interest.

Teachers need to recognize and accept the developmental level of children's writing, which will probably range from those who draw, write strings of letters, invent spelling, to those who are already conventional spellers. Children's writing, including spelling, will develop progressively to higher levels if they are given opportunities to write, read, share their writing and reading, and to interact with teachers and peers about their writing in positive and responsive ways.

WRITING TOPICS

It's better that children be able to select their own topics, rather than to have to write on topics given by the teacher or to complete story starters, or other such "clever" gimmicks. Mary-Martha Rhodes, a third-grade teacher, notes that when children select meaningful topics—topics they know something about and are interested in—they have ownership of the writing and their voices are evident in their writing.

Children derive their topics from several sources. In Mary-Martha's room, they make a list of topics on their writing folders whenever they think of something they might want to write about. Topics emerge for children as they talk and share with one another their interests, ideas, and their writing pieces, and as they read and discuss books. In the beginning, Mary-Martha found it was difficult for some children to select their own topics. But as time progressed, they found it easier as they gained more control over their own writing. Mary-Martha advises: have patience, keep encouraging them, and your goals will be realized.

When given a choice of writing topics, children often choose to write personal narrative. As Calkins (3) said, children write about what is meaningful and real for them. Mary-Martha has noted that her third graders usually write about happenings in their own lives.

Jackie Hughes, a first-grade teacher, also notes that her children usually write personal narrative (see Figure 3-1). In addition, she observes that they will sometimes copy a text (Figure 3-2), retell an incident from a television show or a book (Figure 3-3), make lists of things such as names

37

(Figure 3-4), or label pictures they have drawn (Figure 3-5).

It is exciting to observe children's development in writing. When children write text that has personal meaning, their own voices emerge. They have something to say, and they say it in their own way.

WRITING CONFERENCES

A writing conference is one of the effective ways teachers can use to help children develop their writing. During the conference they discuss the child's writing; the teacher asks questions and makes comments that encourage the child to keep writing. The teacher might make such comments as the following:

Tell me more about what you are saying here.

When you told me about your trip, there were lots of details, but you haven't written very many of those details. Would you like to add anything?

Are you satisfied with this section?

In conducting a writing conference, the teacher has an opportunity to help the child consider what has been written and think of ways to expand or improve the piece if desired. This is best done by focusing on the meaning and clarity of the story rather than on the mechanics of writing.

Another benefit of the writing conference is that children begin to model the same behaviors and questions the teacher has demonstrated. Some third-grade children have peer conferences and small-group conferences. They read or listen to each other's work for appreciation and to raise questions for clarification or to make suggestions for improvement.

Intensive writing conferences probably shouldn't begin until second grade; the beginning writer is usually satisfied with what has been written and isn't ready to engage in any rewriting. The writing conference isn't begun immediately with all children, but rather when children are interested in discussing their writing.

Most teachers improve their writing conferencing techniques with experience. There is no one "right way" to conduct a conference since each teacher and child is different. Some children are sensitive and must be treated carefully, while others readily consider suggestions about ways to improve their writing. Without question, writing conferences—like reading conferences—are well worth the time and effort.

Figure 3-1. Personal narrative.

My dog is funny win
Mommy Thros the bal
She runs ana lep
Like a frog. win she
run and Lepes She
Lokes funny

Figure 3-2. Copy of text.

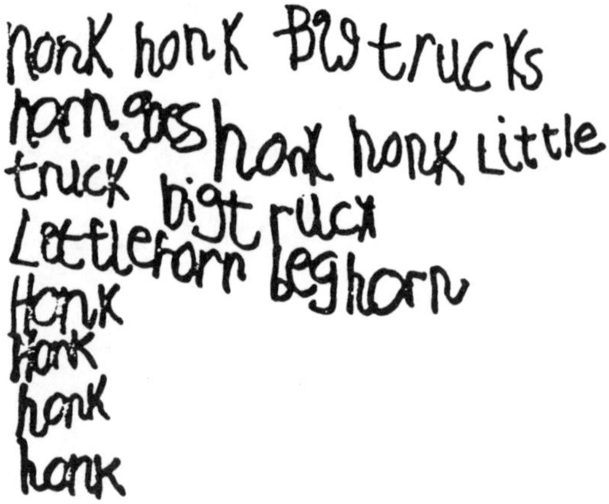

honk honk Big trucks horn goes honk honk Little truck big truck Littlehorn leghorn Honk honk honk honk

Figure 3–3. Retelling of a story.

he Littel boy who
crid wolF wolF
one day a littel boy
was siting up on
a big hill and he
pretindet to pretind

Figure 3–4. List of names.

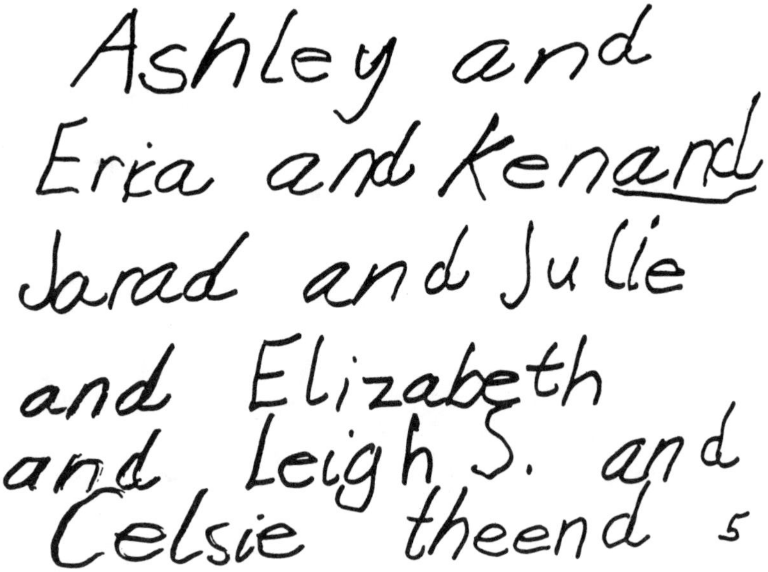

Ashley and
Erica and Kenard
Jarad and Julie
and Elizabeth
and Leigh S. and
Celsie theend 5

Figure 3–5. Labeling a picture.

DICTATION

Many kindergarten and first-grade teachers label their children's pictures by writing on the paper the words, phrases, or sentences the child dictates to them about the picture. Teachers like Lynn Douglas also encourage children to label their own pictures or write a story about their pictures.

While some teachers rotate around the room from child to child, others find it works best for them if they remain at a table and invite children to come to them when they want help or are ready for dictation. Regardless of the way you organize the procedure, it is important to remember that drawing a picture is a good way for young children to rehearse or think about something to write. However, as children become more proficient writers, they no longer need to draw before writing. If they draw something, it is more likely to follow rather than precede their writing.

Many children, especially reluctant writers, profit from being able to dictate their stories. As Allen (1) wrote many years ago, "What I can say, others can write." Dictation has a place in a primary classroom.

Some educators question the use of dictation. Critics say, for instance, that children may become too dependent on the adult to write for them and may not attempt to write themselves. Indeed, this could happen. Furthermore, in dictation the child is not as actively involved in constructing the writing system. Nevertheless, dictation may help some children learn how written language works. For example, Mrs. Hughes, a first-grade teacher, uses dictation as an opening activity each morning. The children give her ideas that they want her to write and she writes their comments on the chalkboard. The dictation remains on the board throughout the day. The children are not asked to copy it, although some choose to do so.

Allen (1) also popularized the writing of group stories. In this activity, children collectively compose a story and the teacher acts as the scribe. In a group of children, there may be those who can write quite well and others who won't attempt to write on their own. Below is an example of a group story.

The Dinosaur Story
Dinosaur means terrible lizard.
Some of the dinosaurs ate plants.
Some of the dinosaurs ate meat.

44

Some dinosaurs lived on land.
Some dinosaurs lived in the water.
Some dinosaurs flew in the air.
Dinosaurs are extinct.
We can see bones of dinosaurs in museums.

Group stories such as this one can be read and enjoyed by the children for the remainder of the school year. The stories can be written on chart paper and displayed or made into a book like the one developed by Mrs. Bagby and her kindergarteners (see Figure 3-6).

Group stories seem especially appropriate following activities that several children have experienced such as retelling a book the teacher has read to the class following a classroom cooking experience. Writing group stories, however, does not replace the writing of individual stories.

JOURNAL WRITING

Journal writing with various formats is now being used by many primary teachers. They may have children write in a spiral notebook or on several sheets of paper stapled together. The actual format of the journal is inconsequential, but it is important to keep the entries together in order to assess growth and have a record of the topics children chose for their entries.

Although the format differs from classroom to classroom, there are some tenets of journal writing that most teachers observe. First and foremost, children select their own content. Teachers do not offer story starters where everyone must write about "a favorite food" or "What I did on my summer vacation." Another point to remember is that journal writing is only a rough draft and neither the mechanics nor content should be graded. A child may wish to do some editing, expanding, or clarifying of content, but it's the child's choice, not the teacher's.

The frequency of journal writing varies from teacher to teacher; some, like Lee Mulch, a third-grade teacher, have daily journal writing and others have it only two or three times a week. The length of time provided for journal writing also varies, although most teachers allow about 10 or 15 minutes. Generally, most younger children would not spend as much time writing in their journals as would older children.

The teacher needs to read the journals of primary children on a fairly

Figure 3–6. A group story by

Mrs. Bagby and her kindergarten class.

Winter is a season.

Sometimes it snows in the winter.

Sometimes we wear mittens and scarves and earmuffs and boots.

We can make snowmen in the winter.

We can ride in a sled.

We can ice skate.

Winter is fun.

The End

regular basis. Some teachers have a written dialogue with their children, responding to the content with comments and questions that often evoke written responses by the children. Some kindergarten and first-grade teachers write in conventional spelling on the backs of the papers what the children say they have written when they draw or write strings of letters. Some teachers feel this is very valuable, but when you work with a large group of such children, it is difficult to do this with each one's writing. At the same time, some teachers tell us that writing down what they say their drawings or letter strings say seems to intimidate some children and may actually inhibit their development as writers.

There is value in having children write every day; their writing as well as their reading improves. Additionally, the journal serves as documentation of a child's progress in writing. Most teachers keep the journals for the entire year and, except for occasional overnight sharing with parents, the journals are not taken home until the end of the year. Parents often point with pride to their child's writing growth evidenced in the journal, and many children readily share what they have written with any adult who will read it or listen to them read it.

DEVELOPMENT IN SPELLING

Children enter school at varying levels of development in writing ability. If teachers ask kindergarten or first-grade children to write the first day of school, they will observe the children who draw pictures, scribble, or make only strings of letters. A few may be able to invent their spelling, reflecting their knowledge of letter-sound correspondence. Ferreiro and Teberosky (7) have given us insights about children's early notions about writing; we encourage the reader to study their work. Our own studies with Constance Kamii provide insights also. In our study of kindergarteners' spelling development, we noted the following levels:

Level 0: Children at this level draw pictures or scribble rather than make letters or symbol-like forms.

Level 1: Children write a string of letters for a word that has no set number of letters from one word to another. The string might run across an entire page as a child spells a word (Figure 3-7).

Level 2: Children write a string of letters that usually consists of three to six letters for each word. The letters may be different for each word or the same letters might be rearranged from one word to the next (Figure 3-8).

Level 3: Children at this level—consonantal level—make letter-sound correspondence, mostly by consonants. For example, they usually write *smt* for cement (Figure 3-9).

Level 4: Children at this level—the alphabetic level—make their letter-sound correspondences by consonants and vowels. For instance, they might write *vacashun* for vacation or *moshun* for motion (Figure 3-10). These consistencies suggest the construction of a system approaching conventional spelling.

Level 5: Children spell most words in the conventional way.

The development of spelling from letter strings to conventional spelling occurs at different times for children. Some make letter strings throughout kindergarten and into first grade and then begin to write at the consonantal level (invented spelling) while others develop to the consonantal level at a very early age. Within each kindergarten class there are likely to be children at each level; however, there may be only a few or none who are conventional spellers.

We are opposed to formal spelling teaching and testing in the early years. Because young children are at such different levels, to insist that those who are at levels 0, 1, 2, or even 3 spell in a conventional way may cause confusion and prevent the child from developing a coherent system of how our written language works. For children at higher levels, spelling is best learned in the context of the writing process.

Henderson (13), Gentry (8), and others have also provided ideas concerning children's spelling development and implications for the teachers of young children. The Annotated Bibliography (pp. 78-80) contains several sources that can be helpful to the teacher who is interested in understanding and supporting the spelling development of his/her children.

Figure 3-7. Level 1.

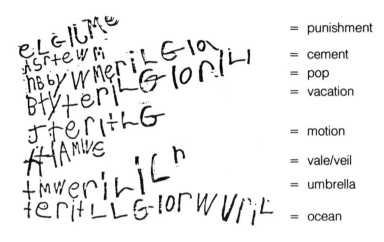

= punishment

= cement
= pop
= vacation

= motion

= vale/veil

= umbrella

= ocean

Figure 3-8. Level 2.

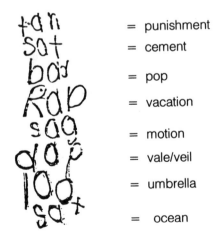

= punishment
= cement

= pop

= vacation

= motion
= vale/veil

= umbrella

= ocean

50

Figure 3–9. Level 3.

Figure 3–10. Level 4.

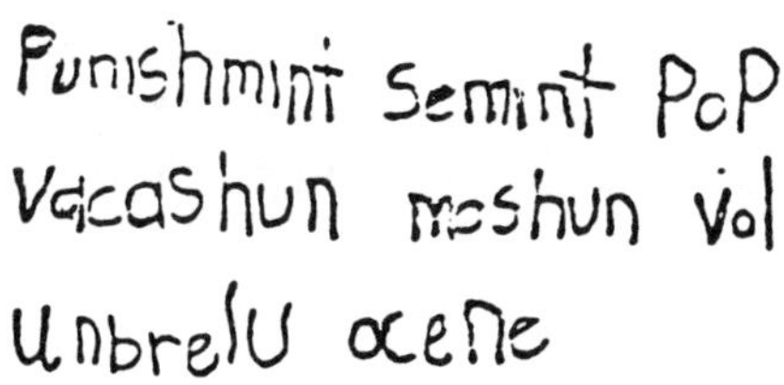

Punishmini semint PoP
Vacashun moshun vol
Unbrelu acene

DEVELOPMENT IN HANDWRITING

Sometimes we forget that handwriting is both for writing and reading, that is, it needs to be legible enough so that others can read it and understand the information and ideas intended by the writer. For the beginning writer, the act of forming letters is a very conscious and sometimes laborious task, requiring a great deal of concentration. As writers become more proficient, the act of handwriting becomes more automatic, requiring less conscious attention.

It is important to provide plenty of practice for young children to write in meaningful ways within the framework of the writing process. In so doing, their handwriting becomes more automatic and their great wish to communicate their ideas to others will underscore for them the importance of writing legibly. It's important to remember that the strong desire to compose information and ideas for others to read is the best motivation for the development of legible handwriting.

Mechanics of Writing

Children must learn the mechanics of writing—punctuation, capitalization, sentence structure, and paragraph construction. In the past, these principles were taught from an English text and from other isolated, fragmented exercises. Many teachers realized that although most children learned these rules and could complete the exercises in the books, they then could not apply them in their writing. Therefore, teachers recognize that these skills are best learned by children in the context of their own writing. When teachers confer with children on later drafts of their writing (conferences on early drafts focus on information), they can focus on a particular element the child is using such as quotation marks. In this way, children learn the mechanics of writing, realize their significance, and become able to apply them in their later writing.

COMPUTERS AND WRITING

Although many educators see computer-assisted instruction as the future of education, we feel there are few good programs to use at the present time. One area that does excite us is word processing. There are several simple word-processing programs currently available for young children. If a computer is available and appropriate software is provided, word processing may facilitate the development of young children's writing abilities. In some schools, each child has a personal disc and keyboard classes are given. Some children have already learned how to use the computer either in community education programs or computer camps. The computer should not take the place of paper and pencil. However, if possible, children should be given the opportunity to learn and use the computer.

ASSESSING DEVELOPMENT OF WRITERS

It's important for teachers to assess the writing development of young children. Teachers, like Fran Davis Perkins who is a first-grade teacher, document writing development in several ways. First, through children's daily journal entries where you can see the child's development over time; this comparison is useful to the teacher, the child, and the parents.

Fran also documents children's writing growth by using writing collected and kept in folders. Each child in her room has a writing folder that contains first drafts and some edited pieces. The pieces are dated and through studying them, teachers, administrators, and parents can observe the writing growth and note the strengths that the child brings to the writing process. The child, too, can see his or her progress by comparing the writing over time.

Laurie Bulgarella, a second-grade teacher, learns a lot about children's writing development through individual conferences. She focuses her attention on the child's growth in expressing ideas clearly and meaningfully. She has found that most of her children start to use the correct mechanics of language through the process of writing; they rarely need instruction on specific skills. Laurie, like other teachers, is an active observer of her children, paying attention to how and what they write so that she can respond in ways that may help to strengthen them as writers.

In a discussion of writing assessment, the issue of grading usually arises. We do not believe in giving grades to children in the primary years; we find it beneficial to use other more meaningful reporting systems. But the fact is, many of you do have to give grades. If you have to grade writing, we suggest that you grade only children's best papers, letting them have a choice in selecting those polished, edited pieces they want graded. It makes no sense to grade everything children write, for like all of us, they have ups and downs in their writing. In assessing children's writing papers, it is best to use a holistic scoring procedure whereby the whole piece of writing is assessed, with emphasis on content, and not on the mechanics such as spelling and punctuation. For more information about assessment and evaluation of writing, we refer the reader to other publications such as *Measures for Research and Evaluation in the English Language Arts* (6), and *A Procedure for Writing Assessment and Holistic Scoring* (19).

WRITING ACROSS THE CURRICULUM

Writing is a means of constructing knowledge and children need to write not only to improve their writing, but also to clarify their thinking. In the process of writing, one must decide what to write about, how to organize ideas, and may, as a result, make new relationships.

As soon as primary children invent their own spelling, often in kindergarten, it is appropriate to ask them to write a statement about what they have learned. Many teachers have a large stack of strips of paper on which children write content information or, of course, they may use large sheets of paper or a notebook. With the strip of paper, however, the child can feel comfortable writing only a few words or a sentence or two.

Learning logs can be used with many second and third graders; they may make daily entries or record as often as they want or as the teacher suggests. Logs used for science, social studies, or math give children an opportunity to ask questions, to make statements about information they have learned, or to make illustrations and label them. Learning logs—like journals—can be spiral notebooks or sheets of paper stapled together.

TRANSFORMING THE EXISTING LANGUAGE ARTS CURRICULUM

Teachers in many schools are given language arts textbooks and/or explicit curriculum guides and are expected to use them. This makes it difficult for those who want to use a more integrated approach in teaching. Fortunately, there are many school administrators who allow or encourage teachers to use their professional knowledge and creativity to plan the curriculum and to teach in the way they feel is best for their students. In some schools, all a teacher needs to do is ask if she/he may depart from the prescribed curriculum or the language arts book and the school principal often will support a teacher with needed resources.

In other schools, administrators discourage such individuality and it requires the teacher's ingenuity to implement a different approach in such a situation. In these schools, there is usually a list of objectives or so-called skills lists that are to be taught at certain grade levels and at designated times of the year. Although it is not easy to meet such requirements and still use your own practices, it can be done to varying degrees. For example, if you are required to teach punctuation such as the use of a period at a certain time of the year, check the children's own writing to see which of them are already using periods and ask the others, in writing conferences, where they think they might need a period.

Each teacher must decide how she or he can make time for meaningful writing activities. We know this can be done.

Chapter 4
FINAL COMMENTS

Teachers who understand whole-language theory recognize the value of natural language learning and oppose a "bits and pieces" curriculum. They are not satisfied with the skills approach they are told to use, and modify the required mandates of their school systems by using many of the practices discussed in this publication.

Teachers must view themselves as professionals and, ideally, should have enough autonomy to develop their own literacy program based on an understanding of how language develops. In the real world of classrooms, there are often rigid guidelines imposed by district policies, state department educational improvement plans, and other external groups. The recent movements often urged as a way to "excellence" unfortunately have decreased excellence in many situations. For example, children are often busy studying *about* reading and writing and focusing on specific skills rather than actually practicing reading and writing in meaningful ways. Teachers are often measured by "time on-task" as defined by "managers" who impose inappropriate tasks on primary children in the name of school improvement. We wish these movements were history in our schools, but many of them are alive and well. Teachers struggle to mark all of the checklists, cover all of the books and workbooks, and prepare children to "bubble" in the right circles on the never-ending tests.

We continue to search for answers to this question: How can a whole-language program based on sound theory and research be implemented in our schools? All of us need to continue to find ways to rethink existing practices and provide learning environments that make learning to read and write more meaningful for children.

Growth of teachers depends to a large extent on their professional autonomy (self-directedness and the ability to make appropriate professional decisions about their literacy programs). Teachers who are autonomous can make professional decisions about their own best kind of literacy program for the particular children under their guidance.

GROWING AS "CHILD WATCHERS"

Kenneth Goodman often says, "Everything I know about reading I learned from children." Being a child watcher means observing children: their language, the meanings they make, their likes and dislikes, their patterns of working and playing with each other, and their growth as thinkers, readers, and writers. Careful child watching can help teachers support children in their natural development as readers and writers.

In our professional development as child watchers, we have benefited greatly from association with several people. Yetta and Ken Goodman and Dorothy Watson have given us their ideas gained from years of child watching. A colleague at the University of Alabama in Birmingham, Constance Kamii, has added greatly to our understanding of Piaget's theory, helping us to understand how children construct knowledge.

ENJOYING CHILDREN'S BOOKS

To see children read with pleasure is a goal of the caring teacher. Throughout this publication, children's literature has been emphasized as being the heart of the reading program. Teachers who enjoy children's books, and their authors and illustrators, help children become excited about them. Helping children explore books they might find interesting is enhanced by the teacher's knowledge about books.

LOOKING FOR AUTHENTIC LITERACY ACTIVITIES

Teachers have to be constantly on the alert for authentic literacy activities that are of interest to children. If basal readers and workbooks are required, you are encouraged to use them in a flexible and creative fashion. Teachers observe that the more they build on the real interests of children, the more exciting the classroom becomes and authentic activities seem to emerge.

INCREASING SOCIAL INTERACTION

Since children learn from each other, it is incumbent upon teachers to maximize the amount of social interaction between and among their

ecially difficult for many teachers because of the
~~belief that a good~~ classroom is a quiet one. We believe that social
interaction in a classroom is essential for learning.

If you fear that chaotic conditions will result from children interacting
with one another, then you will have to struggle to overcome this road-
block. Try stretching yourself in this area a little at a time. For many, it
takes some experience before they become comfortable with children's
interaction.

INTEGRATING THE PROGRAM

Knowledge is not segmented into neat little boxes as some curriculums suggest. Having a period for each subject may make some educators
and parents believe that children have a balanced curriculum, but in
reality these artificial time and subject barriers often get in the way of
learning and, in fact, narrow the curriculum. Reading, writing, listening,
speaking, and thinking cannot be separated and taught as entities in
themselves. Every science and social studies activity has opportunities for
teaching math, literature, writing, reading, and the other language arts.

JOINING TOGETHER

When you approach teaching in new ways, it is helpful to work with
others. Many teachers in the United States and Canada have started their
own support groups. The Goodmans in Tucson, Arizona, and Dorothy
Watson in Columbia, Missouri, first started such groups for teachers
applying whole language (TAWL). They meet together for support and
to learn more about literacy development and how to enhance the language learning of children. There are, of course, other less formal groups
that provide an opportunity for teachers to share their language views
and support one another, and to continue to grow as teachers of whole
language. Professional groups such as the National Council of Teachers
of English, the International Reading Association, and the National
Education Association, and others provide such support for teachers interested in whole-language programs.

If you are the only whole-language teacher in your school, we encourage you to look for a support group to join or to seek teachers in other schools to form such a group. Adults, like children, increase their learning through social interaction.

WORKING AGAINST STANDARDIZATION OF CURRICULUM AND TEACHING

Some educators support a standardized curriculum, having the notion that what is good for one is good for all. While a standardized curriculum may not either greatly benefit or harm many more advanced children, many who are less advanced are likely to lose confidence in their abilities when given instruction that does not make sense to them.

Children need to learn to read and write in order to develop fully, to function and contribute to our democratic society. However, children are developmentally different and should not be branded as failures if they don't learn to read by Christmas of first grade.

In addition to minimizing the standardization of curriculum, we urge teachers to minimize the standardization of teaching approaches. The individual and unique characteristics and strengths of teachers are often overlooked when they are asked to teach a lesson in the same way as all other teachers, as if there is only one right teaching approach. Some systemwide and statewide teacher evaluation systems have teachers scrambling to look alike. We believe that many of these systems have become the enemy of both teachers and children. Teachers must not be forced into rigid models of teaching, but instead should be encouraged to develop their own approaches consistent with their knowledge of what will best serve the interests and development of their children.

WORKING FOR MORE TEACHER AUTONOMY

Teachers inevitably have to make curriculum decisions in their classrooms. It's important that we work together for the autonomy of teachers, encouraging them to be self-directed and responsibly competent, for without these characteristics, professionalism is not possible. Teachers who slavishly follow the dictates of others, who do not know the children in their rooms or who think that children should complete predetermined content outlined in a book, are neither autonomous nor professional. When forced to follow such dictates, many teachers and children become bored and passive about their reading and writing programs.

Teacher autonomy is a key issue in developing a literacy program built on the interests and needs of children. If we work together at all levels of the profession, meaningful and effective reading and writing programs can become a reality.

Appendix A
SOME OF OUR FAVORITE BOOKS*

PICTURE BOOKS

Alexander and the Terrible, Horrible, No Good, Very Bad Day. Judith Viorst. Illustrated by Ray Cruz. New York: Atheneum, 1976.

Alexander and the Wind-up Mouse. Leo Lionni. New York: Pantheon Books, 1969.

Alistair's Elephant. Marilyn Sadler. Illustrated by Roger Bollen. Englewood Cliffs, N.J.: Prentice Hall, 1983.

Amelia Bedalia. Peggy Parish. New York: Harper and Row, 1963; Scholastic, 1970.

The Aminal. Lorna Balian. Nashville, Tenn.: Abingdon Press, 1972.

Animal Fact: Animal Fable. Seymour Simon. New York: Crown, 1979.

Anno's Counting Book. Anno Mitsumasa. New York: Harper, 1977.

Bed Time for Frances. Russell Hoban. Illustrated by Garth Williams. New York: Harper, 1960.

Big Bad Bruce. Bill Peet. Boston: Houghton Mifflin, 1953.

The Biggest Bear. Lynd Ward. Boston: Houghton Mifflin, 1977.

Blueberries for Sal. Robert McCloskey. New York: Viking Press, 1948; Puffin, 1976.

Brown Bear, Brown Bear, What Do You See? Bill Martin. Illustrated by Eric Carle. New York: Holt, Rinehart and Winston, 1967.

The Cat's Power. Ashley Bryan. New York: Atheneum, 1985.

A Chair for My Mother. Vera Williams. New York: Greenwillow Books, 1982.

Corduroy. Don Freeman. New York: Viking Press, 1968; Puffin, 1976.

---

*For easy accessibility, books in the Appendix are listed alphabetically by title.

Could Be Worse! James Stevenson. New York: Greenwillow Books, 1977.

Crow Boy. Taro Yashima. New York: Viking Press, 1955.

Curious George. H. A. Rey. Boston: Houghton Mifflin, 1941; 1973.

Drummer Hoff. Barbara Emberley. Illustrated by Ed Emberley. Englewood Cliffs, N.J.: Prentice-Hall, 1967.

Ferdinand. Munro Leaf. Illustrated by Robert Lawson. New York: Puffin Books, 1936.

Frederick. Leo Lionni. New York: Pantheon Books, 1966.

Frederick's Fables. Leo Lionni. New York: Pantheon Books, 1985.

Frog and Toad Are Friends. Arnold Lobel. New York: Harper, 1970; 1979.

The Giving Tree. Shel Silverstein. New York: Harper, 1964.

Grandma's Joy. Eloise Greenfield. Illustrated by Carole Byard. New York: Philomel Books, 1980.

The Grouchy Ladybug. Eric Carle. New York: Thomas Y. Crowell, 1977.

A Hole Is to Dig. Ruth Krauss. Illustrated by Maurice Sendak. New York: Harper, 1952.

Horton Hears a Who. Dr. Seuss. New York: Random House, 1954.

Ira Sleeps Over. Bernard Waber. Boston: Houghton Mifflin, 1972.

The Island of the Skog. Steven Kellogg. New York: Dial Press, 1973.

Jim and the Beanstalk. Raymond Briggs. New York: Coward, McCann and Geoghegan, Inc., 1970.

The Jolly Postman. Janet Ahlberg, and Allan Ahlberg. Boston: Little, Brown, 1986.

Jumanji. Chris Van Allsburg. Boston: Houghton Mifflin, 1981.

King Bidgoods in the Bathtub. Audrey Wood. New York: Harcourt Brace Jovanovich, 1985.

The Knight and the Dragon. Tomie De Paola. New York: G. P. Putnam's Sons, 1980.

Leo the Late Bloomer. Robert Kraus. Illustrated by Jose Aruego. New York: Windmill Books, 1971.

Let's Be Early Settlers with Daniel Boone. Peggy Parish. New York: Harper and Row, 1967.

The Little Engine That Could. Watty Piper. Illustrated by George and Doris Hanman. New York: Platt, 1961; Scholastic, 1979.

Little Red Riding Hood. Retold and illustrated by Trina Schart Hyman. New York: Holiday House, 1983.

Madeline. Ludwig Bemelmans. New York: Viking Press, 1939; Puffin, 1977.

Make Way for Ducklings. Robert McCloskey. New York: Viking Press, 1941; Puffin, 1976.

May I Bring a Friend? Beatrice de Regniers. Illustrated by Beni Montressor. New York: Atheneum, 1964.

Mike Mulligan and His Steam Shovel. Virginia Lee Burton. Boston: Houghton Mifflin, 1939; 1977.

Mr. Willowby's Christmas Tree. Robert Barry. New York: McGraw-Hill, 1963.

My Brother Fine with Me. Lucile Clifton. New York: Holt, Rinehart and Winston, 1975.

Oliver Button Is a Sissy. Tomie de Paola. New York: Harcourt Brace Jovanovich, 1979.

The Pain and the Great One. Judy Blume. New York: Dell, 1974.

Polar Express. Chris Van Allsburg. Boston: Houghton Mifflin, 1986.

Professor Noah's Spaceship. Brian Wildsmith. New York: Oxford University Press, 1980.

Q Is for Duck. Mary Elting, and Michael Folson. Illustrated by Jack Kent. New York: Clarion Books, 1980.

Ramona the Brave. Beverly Cleary. Illustrated by Alan Tiegreen. New York: Morrow, 1975.

Ramona the Pest. Beverly Cleary. New York: Morrow, 1968.

Rosie's Walk. Pat Hutchins. New York: Macmillan, 1968.

Say It! Charlotte Zolotow. Illustratd by James Stevenson. New York: Greenwillow Books, 1980.

She Come Bringing Me That Little Baby Girl. Eloise Greenfield. Illustrated by John Steptoe. Philadelphia: J. B. Lippincott, 1974.

The Snowy Day. Ezra Jack Keats. New York: Viking Press, 1962.

Stevie. John Steptoe. New York: Harper, 1969.

Story of Jumping Mouse. John Steptoe. New York: Lothrop, Lee and Shepard Books, 1984.

Strega Nona. Tomie de Paola. Englewood Cliffs, N.J.: Prentice-Hall, 1975.

Sylvester and the Magic Pebble. William Steig. New York: Simon and Schuster, 1969,

The Tale of Thomas Mead. Pat Hutchins. New York: Greenwillow Books, 1980.

There Was an Old Woman. Stephen Wyllie, and Maureen Roffey. New York: Harper and Row, 1985.

Tikki Tikki Timbo. Arlene Mosel. Illustrated by Blair Lent. New York: Holt, Rinehart and Winston, 1968; Scholastic, 1972.

Where the Wild Things Are. Maurice Sendak. New York: Harper, 1963.

Where's Spot? Eric Hill. New York: Putnam, 1980.

William's Doll. Charlotte Zolotow. Illustrated by William Pine du Bois. New York: Harper, 1972; 1985.

Your First Garden Book. Marc Brown. Boston: Little, Brown, 1981.

BOOKS FOR MORE PROFICIENT READERS (or for reading aloud)

Beat the Story-Drum, Pum-Pum (and numerous other African folk tale books). Retold by Ashley Bryan. New York: Atheneum, 1980.

Ben and Me. Robert Lawson. New York: Dell Publishing Co. (Yearling Book), 1939.

Bunicula. Deborah Howe, and James Howe. New York: Atheneum, 1984.

Charlie and the Chocolate Factory. Roald Dahl. Illustrated by Joseph Schindelman. New York: Alfred A. Knopf, 1964.

Charlotte's Web. E. B. White. Illustrated by Garth Williams. New York: Harper, 1952.

Cricket in Times Square. George Selden. Illustrated by Garth Williams. New York: Farrar, Straus, and Giroux, 1960; 1970.

Did You Carry the Flag Today, Charley? Rebecca Caudill. New York: Holt, Rinehart and Winston, 1971.

A Dog Called Kitty. Bill Wallace. New York: Archway, 1980.

The Enormous Egg. Oliver Butterworth. Boston: Little, Brown, 1956; New York: Dell, 1978.

Fantastic Mr. Fox. Roald Dahl. New York: Alfred A. Knopf, 1970.

Freckle Juice. Judy Blume. New York: Four Winds Press, 1971; Dell, 1971.

Homer Price. Robert McCloskey. New York: Viking Press, 1943; Penguin, 1976.

How to Eat Fried Worms. Thomas Rockwell. New York: Franklin Watts, 1973.

Lentil. Robet McCloskey. New York: Viking Press, 1940.

Lion and the Ostrich Chicks. Retold by Ashley Brian. New York: Atheneum, 1986.

Little House in the Big Woods (and other books in the "Little House" series). Laura Ingalls Wilder. Illustrated by Garth Williams. New York: Harper and Row, 1953.

The Macmillan Book of Greek Gods and Heroes. Alice Low. New York: Macmillan, 1985.

Mama's Going to Buy You a Mockingbird. Jean Little. New York: Viking Press, 1984.

Mr. Popper's Penguins. Richard Atwater, and Florence Atwater. New York: Dell Publishing Co. (Yearling Books), 1938.

Mrs. Piggle-Wiggle's Magic. Betty MacDonald. Philadelphia: J. B. Lippincott, 1949.

Rabbit Hill. Robert Lawson. New York: Viking Press, 1944.

Ramona the Pest (and numerous other books about Ramona and Henry Huggins and others). Beverly Cleary. New York: Morrow, 1968; Dell, 1982.

Sarah, Plain and Tall. Patricia MacLachlan. New York: Harper and Row, 1985.

The Secret Garden. Frances Hodgson Burnett. Illustrated by Tasha Tudor. Philadelphia: J. B. Lippincott, 1962; New York: Dell, 1971.

Seven Kisses in a Row. Patricia MacLachlan. New York: Harper and Row, 1983.

The Sign of the Beaver. Elizabeth George Speare. Boston: Houghton Mifflin, 1983.

A Stranger Came Ashore. Mollie Hunter. New York: Harper and Row, 1975.

The Velveteen Rabbit. Margery Williams. Illustrated by Daniel Jorgenson. New York: Alfred A. Knopf, 1985.

Walk Together Children. Collected by Ashley Bryan. New York: Atheneum, 1974.

Appendix B
A LIST OF POETRY COLLECTIONS

Book of Poetry for Children. Collected by Jack Prelutsky. New York: Random House, 1983.

Bronzeville Boys and Girls. Gwendolyn Brooks. New York: Harper and Row, 1956.

Catch Me and Kiss Me and Say It Again. Clyde Watson. New York: Philomel Books, 1978.

A Circle of Seasons. Myra Cohn Livingston. New York: Holiday House, 1982.

Hailstones and Halibut Bones. Mary O'Neill. New York: Doubleday, 1961.

Honey, I Love. Eloise Greenfield. New York: Thomas Y. Crowell, 1972.

If I Were in Charge of the World. Judith Viorst. New York: Atheneum, 1981.

Kingfisher Book of Childrens' Poetry. Collected by Michael Rosen. London: Kingfisher Books, 1985.

A Light in the Attic. Shel Silverstein. New York: Harper and Row, 1981.

The Malibu and Other Poems. Myra Cohn Livingston. New York: Atheneum, 1972.

Monster Poems. Collected by Daisy Wallace. New York: Holiday House, 1976.

Morning Noon and Night-Time, Too. Collected by Lee Bennett Hopkins. New York: Harper and Row, 1980.

My Black Me. Collected by Arnold Adoff. New York: E. P. Dutton, 1974.

My Daddy Is a Cool Dude. Karama Fufuka. New York: Dial Press, 1975.

New Kid on the Block. Jack Prelutsky. New York: Greenwillow Books, 1984.

On City Streets. Collected by Nancy Larrick. New York: M. Evans and Co., 1968.

Poems Children Will Sit Still For. Collected by Beatrice De Regniers and others. New York: Scholastic Book Service, 1969.

The Sky Is Full of Songs. Collected by Lee Bennett Hopkins. New York: Harper and Row, 1983.

Spin a Soft Black Song. Nikki Giovanni. New York: Hill and Wang, 1985.

Where the Sidewalk Ends. Shel Silverstein. New York: Harper and Row, 1974.

Zero Makes Me Hungry. Collected by Edward Lueders. Glenview, Ill.: Scott, Foresman, 1976.

Appendix C
A LIST OF BIG BOOK PUBLISHERS

Class Size Books Limited
P.O. Box 366
Port Coquitlam,
British Columbia, Canada
V3C 4K6

Gage Publishing Ltd.
164 Consumer Blvd.
Agincourt, Ontario
Canada
MIS 3C7

Ginn and Company
191 Spring Street
Lexington, MA 02173

Holt, Rinehart and Winston
383 Madison Avenue
New York, NY 10017

Rigby Education
454 S. Virginia Street
Crystal Lake, IL 60014

Scholastic, Inc.
P.O. Box 7502
Jefferson City, MO 65102

Scott, Foresman and Company
1900 East Lake Avenue
Glenview, IL 60025

The Wright Group
10949 Technology Place
P.O. Box 27780
San Diego, CA 92127

Appendix D
A LIST OF BOOKS USED FOR COOKING AS AN EXTENDING ACTIVITY

Arthur's Christmas Cookie. Lillian Hoban. New York: Harper and Row, 1972.

The Blueberry Cake That Little Fox Baked. Andrew Da Rif. New York: Atheneum, 1984.

The Cookie Tree. Jay Williams. New York: Parents Magazine Press, 1967.

Cranberry Thanksgiving. Wende Devlin, and Harry Devlin. New York: Parents Magazine Press, 1971.

Dragon Stew. Tom McGowen. Illustrated by Trina Schart Hyman. Chicago: Follett Publishing, 1969.

The Duchess Bakes a Cake. Virginia Kahl. New York: Charles Scribner's Sons, 1955.

George Washington's Breakfast. Jean Fritz. New York: Coward-McCann, 1969.

The Giant Jam Sandwich. John Vernon Lord. Boston: Houghton Mifflin, 1973.

The Gingerbread Man. Jan Sukus. Racine, Wis.: Western Publishing Co., 1969.

The Guest. James Marshall. Boston: Houghton Mifflin, 1975.

Gus Was a Friendly Ghost. Gus Thayer. Illustrated by Seymour Fleishman. New York: William Morrow, 1962.

Homer Price, "The Doughnuts." Robert McCloskey. New York: Viking Press, 1943.

How to Make Possum's Honey Bread. Carla Stevens. Illustrated by Jack Kent. New York: The Seabury Press, 1975.

In the Night Kitchen. Maurice Sendak. New York: Harper and Row, 1970.

Journey Cake, Ho! Keith Sawyer. New York: Viking Press, 1953.

Little Bear Learns to Read the Cookbook. Janice Brustlein. Illustrated by Marian Foster Curtis. New York: Lothrop, Lee and Shepard, 1969.

More Potatoes. Millicent Selsam. New York: Harper and Row, 1972.

Pancakes for Breakfast. Tomie de Paola. New York: Harcourt Brace Jovanovich, 1975.

The Popcorn Book. Tomie de Paola. New York: Holiday House, 1978.

Poppy Seed Cakes. Margery Clark. New York: Doubleday, 1924.

The Pretzel Hero. Barbara Rinkoff. New York: Parents Magazine Press, 1970.

The Queen Who Couldn't Bake Gingerbread. Dorothy Van Woerkom. New York: Alfred A. Knopf, 1975.

Rain Makes Applesauce. Julian Scheer. New York: Holiday House, 1964.

SAM. Ann Herbert Scott. Illustrated by Symeon Shimin. New York: McGraw-Hill, 1967.

The Search for Delicious. Natalie Babbit. New York: Farrar, Straus and Giroux, 1969.

Stone Soup. Marcia Brown. New York: Charles Scribner's Sons, 1947.

Sylvester and the Magic Pebble. William Steig. New York: Windmill Books, 1969.

Walter the Baker. Eric Carle. New York: Alfred A. Knopf, 1972.

Appendix E
A LIST OF PREDICTABLE BOOKS

The Aminal. Lorna Balian. Nashville, Tenn.: Abingdon Press, 1972.

The Ants Go Marching. B. Freschet. New York: Charles Scribner's Sons, 1973.

Are You My Mother? P. D. Eastman. Don Mills, Ont.: William Collins Sons, 1960.

Brown Bear, Brown Bear. Bill Martin. New York: Holt, Rinehart and Winston, 1970.

The Bus Ride. Illustrated by J. Wager. Glenview, Ill: Scott, Foresman, 1971.

Catch a Little Fox. Beatrice de Regniers. New York: Seabury Press, 1970.

Chicken Soup with Rice. Maurice Sendak. New York: Harper, 1962.

Crocodile and Hen. Joan Lenax. New York: Harper and Row, 1969.

Drummer Hoff Adapted. Barbara Emberley. Illustrated by Ed Emberley. Englewood Cliffs, N.J.: Prentice-Hall, 1967.

Each Peach, Pear Plum. J. Allenberg, and A. Allenberg. New York: Viking Press, 1978.

Elephant in a Well. Marie Hall Ets. New York: Viking Press, 1972.

The Fat Cat. Jack Kent. New York: Scholastic, 1971.

Fire! Fire! Said Mrs. McGuire. Bill Martin. New York: Holt, Rinehart and Winston, 1970.

Flower Pot Is Not a Hat. Martha Moffett. New York: E. P. Dutton, 1972.

Fortunately. Remy Charlip. New York: Four Winds Press, 1964.

Frog Went A-Courtin'. John Langstaff. New York: Harcourt Brace Jovanovich, 1955.

Go Tell Aunt Rhody. Aliki. New York: Macmillan, 1974.

Goodnight Moon. Margaret Wise Brown. New York: Harper and Row, 1947.

Goodnight Owl. Pat Hutchins. New York: Macmillan, 1972.

The Great Big Enormous Turnip. A. Tolstoy. New York: Franklin Watts, 1968.

The Grouchy Lady Bug. Eric Carle. New York: Thomas Y. Crowell, 1977.

The Haunted House. Bill Martin. New York: Holt, Rinehart and Winston, 1970.

House Is a House for Me. Mary Ann Hoberman. New York: Viking Press, 1978.

Hush, Little Baby. Margot Zemach, New York: E. P. Dutton, 1976.

I Know an Old Lady Who Swallowed a Fly. Nadine Bernard Wescott. Boston: Little, Brown, 1980.

I Love Ladybugs. R. Van Allen. Allen, Tex.: DLM Teaching Resources, 1985.

I Once Knew a Man. F. Brandenberg. New York: Macmillan, 1970.

I Was Walking Down the Road. Sarah Barahas. New York: Scholastic, 1975.

It Looked Like Spilt Milk. Charles Shaw. New York: Harper and Row, 1947.

Just for You. Mercer Mayer. New York: Golden Books, 1975.

Just Like Daddy. Frank Asch. Englewood Cliffs, N.J.: Prentice-Hall, 1981.

King Rooster, Queen Hen. Anita Lobel. New York: Greenwillow Books, 1975.

Klippety Klop. Ed Emberley. Boston: Little, Brown, 1974.

The Little Red Hen. Paul Galdone. New York: Scholastic, 1973.

May I Bring a Friend? Beatrice de Regniers. New York: Atheneum, 1974.

Monkey Face. Frank Asch. New York: Parents Magazine Press, 1977.

Mother, Mother I Want Another. Maria Polushkin. New York: Crown, 1978.

The Napping House. Audrey Wood, and Don Wood. New York: Harcourt Brace Jovanovich, 1984.

Oh, A-Hunting We Will Go. John Langstaff. New York: Atheneum, 1974.

One Monday Morning. Uri Shulevitz. New York: Charles Scribner's Sons, 1967.

One, Two, Three, Goes the Sea. Alain. New York: Scholastic, 1964.

Over in the Meadow. Ezra Jack Keats. New York: Scholastic, 1971.

Rain Makes Applesauce. J. Scheer, and M. Bileck. New York: Holiday House, 1964.

The Rose in My Garden. Arnold Lobel. New York: Scholastic, 1984.

Rosie's Walk. Pat Hutchens. New York: Macmillan, 1968.

Rum Pum Pum. Maggie Duff. New York: Macmillan, 1978.

Seven Little Rabbits. John Becker. New York: Scholastic, 1973.

She'll Be Comin' Round the Mountain. Robert Quackenbush. Philadelphia: J. B. Lippincott, 1973.

Skip to My Lou. Robert Quackenbush. Philadelphia: J. B. Lippincott, 1975.

The Snow Child. F. Littledale. New York: Scholastic, 1978.

Someone Is Eating the Sun. Ruth Sonneborn. New York: Random House, 1974.

The Teeny Tiny Woman. Margot Zemach. New York: Scholastic, 1965.

Ten Little Animals. Carl Memling. New York: Golden Books, 1961.

Ten, Nine, Eight. M. Baug. New York: William Morrow, 1983.

The Three Billy Goats Gruff. Marcia Brown. New York: Harcourt Brace Jovanovich, 1957.

The Three Little Pigs. P. Geldone. New York: Seabury Press, 1970.

Titch. Pat Hutchens. New York: Collier Books, 1971.

Too Much Noise. A. McGovern. New York: Scholastic, 1967.

Treeful of Pigs. Arnold Lobel. New York: Greenwillow Books, 1979.

Turtle Tale. F. Asch. New York: Dial Press, 1978.

Twelve Days of Christmas. Brian Wildsmith. New York: Franklin Watts, 1972.

Upside Down Day. Julian Scheer and Marvin Bileck. New York: Holiday House, 1968.

The Very Busy Spider. Eric Carle. New York: Philomel Books, 1984.

The Very Hungry Caterpillar. Eric Carle. New York: Philomel Books, 1981.

The Visit. Diane Wolkstein. New York: Alfred A. Knopf, 1977.

We're Off to Catch a Dragon. Ester Laurence. Nashville, Tenn.: Abingdon Press, 1969.

What Do You Do with a Kangaroo? Mercer Mayer. New York: Scholastic, 1973.

When I First Came to This Land. Oscar Barnd. New York: Putnam's Sons, 1974.

Where Did My Mother Go? Edna Mitchell Preston. New York: Four Winds Press, 1978.

Whose Mouse Are You? Robert Kraus. New York: Collier Books, 1970.

Why Can't I Fly? R. Gelman. New York: Scholastic, 1976.

BIBLIOGRAPHY

1. Allen, Roach Van. *Language Experiences in Communication.* Boston: Houghton Mifflin, 1976.
2. _____. *I Love Ladybugs.* Allen, Tex.: DLM Teaching Resources, 1985.
3. Calkins, Lucy. *The Art of Teaching Writing.* Portsmouth, N.H.: Heinemann Educational Books, 1986.
4. Carle, Eric. *The Grouchy Ladybug.* New York: Thomas Y. Crowell, 1971.
5. Credle, Ellis. *Down, Down the Mountain.* Camden, N.J.: Nelson, 1934.
6. Fagan, William T.; Cooper, Charles R.; and Jensen, Julie M. *Measures for Research and Evaluation in the English Language Arts.* Urbana, Ill.: National Council of Teachers of English, 1975.
7. Ferreiro, Emilia, and Teberosky, Ana. *Literacy Before Schooling.* Exeter, N.H.: Heinemann Educational Books, 1982.
8. Gentry, J. Richard. "You Can Analyze Developmental Spelling and Here's How To Do It." *Early Years* 15 (May 1985): 44-45.
9. Goodman, Kenneth; Smith, E. Brooks; Meredith, Robert; and Goodman, Yetta M. 3d ed. *Language and Thinking in School—A Whole-Language Curriculum.* New York: Richard C. Owens Publishers, 1987.
10. Goodman, Yetta, and Burke, Carolyn. *Reading Strategies: Focus on Comprehension.* New York: Richard C. Owens Publishers, 1980.
11. Goodman, Yetta; Watson, Dorothy; and Burke, Carolyn. *Reading Miscue Inventory.* New York: Richard C. Owens Publishers, 1987.
12. Graves, Donald. *Writing: Teachers and Children at Work.* Portsmouth, N.H.: Heinemann Educational Books, 1983.
13. Henderson, Edmund. *Teaching Spelling.* Boston: Houghton Mifflin, 1985.
14. Hipple, Marjorie L. "Journal Writing in Kindergarten." *Language Arts* 62 (March 1985): 255-61.
15. Holdaway, Don. *The Foundations of Literacy.* Exeter, N.H.: Heinemann Educational Books, 1979.
16. Lionni, Leo. *Frederick.* New York: Pantheon Books, 1967.
17. Long, Roberta; Manning, Maryann; and Manning, Gary. "One-on-One on Reading." *Teaching K-9* 17 (February 1987): 59-62.
18. Melser, June, and Cowley, Joy. *In a Dark Dark Wood.* San Diego: The Wright Group Co., 1980.
19. Myers, Miles. *A Procedure for Writing Assessment and Holistic Scoring.* Urbana, Ill.: National Council of Teachers of English, 1980.

76

20. Roberts, Elizabeth Madox. "The Woodpecker." In *Arbuthnot Anthology of Children's Literature*, edited by May Hill, p. 52. Glenview, Ill.: Scott, Foresman, 1961.
21. Rye, James. *Cloze Procedure and the Teaching of Reading*. Exeter, N.H.: Heinemann Educational Books, 1982.
22. Steig, William. *Sylvester and the Magic Pebble*. New York: Windmill Books, 1969.
23. Tchudi, Stephen N., and Tchudi, Susan J. *Teaching Writing in the Content Areas: Elementary School*. Washington, D.C.: National Education Association, 1983.
24. White, E. B. *Charlotte's Web*. Illustrated by Garth Williams. New York: Harper, 1952.
25. _____. *Stuart Little*. Illustrated by Garth Williams. New York: Harper, 1945.
26. _____. *The Trumpet of the Swan*. Illustrated by Edward Frascino. New York: Harper, 1920.

ANNOTATED BIBLIOGRAPHY

Bussis, Anne M.; Chittenden, Edward A.; Amarel, Marianne; and Klausner, Edith. *Inquiring into Meaning—An Investigation of Learning to Read*. Hillsdale, N.J.: Lawrence Erlbaum Associates, 1985.
    Presents important findings and theoretical outcomes of a six-year investigation of young children learning to read. The reports of the studies provide the reader with a better understanding of how young children become literate.

Butler, Andrea, and Turbill, Jan. *Towards a Reading-Writing Classroom*. Rozelle, Australia: Primary English Teaching Association, 1984.
    The authors give a theoretical background to the reading-writing process and relate the theory to practice. They emphasize immersing children in print, involving them in writing, and helping them to make the connections between reading and writing.

Calkins, Lucy M. *The Art of Teaching Writing*. Portsmouth, N.H.: Heinemann Educational Books, 1986.
    Calkins shares her views about teaching writing in language arts and across the curriculum. The descriptions of writing development and suggestions for teaching writing at each grade level are very useful. The book reflects her excellent style as a writer, which makes the reader want to keep on reading.

Clay, Marie. *What Did I Write?* Exeter, N.H.: Heinemann Educational Books, 1975.
    A collection of children's work with comments about the implications of the work. Clay emphasizes the relationship of early writing to early reading.

Farr, Roger. *Reading: Trends and Challenges*. 2d ed. Washington, D.C.: National Education Association, 1986.
    An excellent and brief review of selected reading research and the status of reading in the United States. Farr emphasizes the idea that the teacher is still the key to reading instruction.

Ferreiro, Emilia, and Teberosky, Ana. *Literacy Before Schooling*. Exeter, N.H.: Heinemann Educational Books, 1982.
    Using a Piagetian approach for studying children's literacy development, the authors show how children construct a written language system. Teachers interested in young children's literacy development will want to put this book on their "must read" list.

Goodman, Kenneth. *What's Whole in Whole Language*. Portsmouth, N.H.: Heinemann Educational Books, 1986.

This easy-to-read book describes the whole-language movement. It addresses language development and reading and writing development. Also provides suggestions for helping children become literate, using examples of successful whole-language programs.

Goodman, Kenneth S.; Smith, E. Brooks; Meredith, Robert; and Goodman, Yetta M. *Language and Thinking in School—A Whole-Language Curriculum*. 3d ed. New York: Richard C. Owen Publishers, 1987.

The authors discuss the relationships among language, thought processes, and education and provide ways to build and assess curriculum and instruction. The book reflects the extensive developments that have occurred in the areas of language and thinking during the past decade. It is essential reading for those interested in a scientific view of education, rather than a behavioristic-mechanistic one. The authors emphasize the fact that teachers need a base of knowledge and theory in order to help their students develop.

Holdaway, Don. *Stability and Change in Literacy Learning*. Portsmouth, N.H.: Heinemann Educational Books, 1984.

This very concise book provides excellent summaries of useful and relevant research of reading and writing instruction. Addresses environment, programs, and teaching practices.

Holdaway, Don. *The Foundations of Literacy*. Exeter, N.H.: Heinemann Educational Books, 1979.

The author, using a developmental perspective, gives clear and sound ideas for teaching young children to read and write. Included is a meaningful and helpful discussion about shared book experiences.

Newkirk, Thomas, and Atwell, Nancie, eds. *Understanding Writing*. Chelmsford, Mass.: Northeast Regional Exchange, 1982.

A collection of articles dealing with beginning writing, conferences, writing and reading relationships, and assessment. Insights are given about ways children learn to write, and how classroom teachers can help them.

Newman, Judith M., ed. *Whole Language—Theory in Use*. Portsmouth, N.H.: Heinemann Educational Books, 1985.

Provides specific ideas for teaching reading and writing from a whole-language perspective and for creating meaningful literacy environments in which children are active in their own learning. Specific areas addressed include children's books, journal writing, spelling, and conferencing.

Rye, James. *Cloze Procedure and the Teaching of Reading.* Exeter, N.H.: Heinemann Educational Books, 1982.
> A discussion of several aspects of the cloze procedure including psychology of reading process, readability measurement, reading development, reading diagnosis, testing, and content reading. Especially helpful are the ideas for using cloze to improve children's reading comprehension.

Sampson, Michael R. *The Pursuit of Literacy, Early Reading and Writing.* Dubuque, Iowa: Kendall Hunt, 1986.
> A collection of articles by well-known literacy teachers and researchers. Includes articles on the foundations of literacy, literacy learning in schools, and curriculum implications for literacy learning. It is a book well worth reading.

Tchudi, Stephen N., and Tchudi, Susan J. *Teaching Writing in the Content Areas: Elementary School.* Washington, D.C.: National Education Association, 1983.
> Provides ideas for content area writing, including procedures for lesson plans, model units, topics, and evaluation and grading. The authors emphasize the importance of keeping content at the center of the writing process and give suggestions for doing so.

Temple, Charles A.; Nathan, Ruth G.; and Burris, Nancy A. *The Beginnings of Writing.* Boston: Allyn and Bacon, 1982.
> Presents early scribbling behaviors of young children and discusses the developmental levels of children's spelling. In addition to the excellent discussion of spelling development, the authors provide insights about forms of composition of young children.

Thaiss, Christopher. *Language Across the Curriculum in the Elementary Grades.* Urbana, Ill.: National Council of Teachers of English, 1986.
> Reviews research findings related to the approach of language across the curriculum. The author shows how speaking, writing, listening, and reading are used to teach content. Activities suggested include logs, journals, games, and small-group discussion.